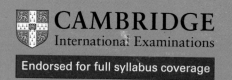

CAMBRIDGE
International Examinations

Endorsed for full syllabus coverage

Complete English for Cambridge Secondary 1

7

Series editor: Dean Roberts
Alan Jenkins
Tony Parkinson

OXFORD
UNIVERSITY PRESS

OXFORD
UNIVERSITY PRESS

Great Clarendon Street, Oxford, OX2 6DP, United Kingdom

Oxford University Press is a department of the University of Oxford. It furthers the University's objective of excellence in research, scholarship, and education by publishing worldwide. Oxford is a registered trade mark of Oxford University Press in the UK and in certain other countries

British Library Cataloguing in Publication Data

Data available

978-0-19-836465-8

1 3 5 7 9 10 8 6 4 2

MIX
Paper from responsible sources
FSC C007785

Paper used in the production of this book is a natural, recyclable product made from wood grown in sustainable forests. The manufacturing process conforms to the environmental regulations of the country of origin.

Printed in Great Britain by Bell and Bain Ltd., Glasgow

Acknowledgements

The publishers would like to thank the following for permissions to use their photographs:

Cover image: David Newton/Bridgeman Art; p2: andreiuc88/Shutterstock; p2l: inhauscreative/Getty Images; p2R: Tiberiu Sahlean/Shutterstock; p3t: Dennis W. Donohue/Shutterstock; p3m: © Bettmann/Corbis/Image Library; p3b: Jordan Siemens/Iconica/Getty Images; p4: Greg Epperson/Shutterstock; p7: Jim Cummins/The Image Bank/Getty Images; p8: Cadence Moore/Shutterstock; p12: Corbis/Image Library; p16: Roberto Caucino/Shuttersock; p13: aodaodaodaod/Shutterstock; p18: Paket/Shutterstock; p18l: © Thomas Hartwell/CORBIS/Image Library; p18r: © Marijan Murat/dpa/Corbis/Image Library; p20: tomtsya/Shutterstock; p21: © Carmen Redondo/CORBIS/Image Library; p25: Cienpies Design/Shutterstock; p28: Julie Dermansky/Science Source/Getty Images; p29: Dmytro Balkhovitin/Shutterstock; p30: © Thierry Tronnel/Corbis/Image Library; p32: Robert Adrian Hillman/Shutterstock; p34: Patrick Poendl/Shutterstock; p48: Paolo Bona/Shutterstock; p34l: Anadolu Agency/Getty Images; p34r: Bikeworldtravel/Shutterstock; p35: PRAKASH SINGH/AFP/Getty Images; p38a: Kuznetcov_Konstantin/Shutterstock; p38b: Rostislav Ageev/Shutterstock; p38c: Sira Anamwong/Shutterstock; p40: © Robert Holmes/CORBIS/Image Library; p41t: Smit/Shutterstock; p41b: aastock/Shutterstock; p43l: Maria Galan / Alamy Stock Photo; p43r: Shutterstock; p45: Jakkrit Orrasri/Shutterstock; p50: Serg64/Shutterstock; p50l: Dudarev Mikhail/Shutterstock; p50r: Artem Zhushman/Shutterstock; p52: Fanfo/Shutterstock; p54b: EpicStockMedia/Shutterstock; p54t: SnowWhiteimages/Shutterstock; p59: The Visual Explorer/Shutterstock; p60l: Przemyslaw Skibinski/Shutterstock; p60r:

Anton_Ivanov/Shutterstock; p64: Fanfo/Shutterstock; p66l: Daniel Prudek/Shutterstock; p66r: lculig/Shutterstock; p72tl: Volt Collection/Shutterstock; p72tr: Teo Boon Keng Alvin/Shutterstock; p72bl: Asia Images/Shutterstock; p72br: Pius Lee/Shutterstock; p73tl: AJP/Shutterstock; p73tr: 1000 Words/Shutterstock; p76: Maxim Petrichuk/Shutterstock; p80: Shutterstock; p81: Shutterstock; P66: Jorg Hackemann/Shutterstock; P82: Mondadori Portfolio/Getty Images; p82l: Mondadori Portfolio/Getty Images; p82r: The Asahi Shimbun/Getty Images; p83: racorn/Shutterstock; p84: © John Springer Collection/CORBIS/Image Library; p87: f9photos/Shutterstock; p88: © Robbie Jack/Corbis/Image Library; p92: Amoret Tanner / Alamy Stock Photo; p93: © Michael Nicholson/Corbis/Image Library; p95: Ulrich Doering / Alamy Stock Photo; p96: cosma/Shutterstock; p98: IM_photo/Shutterstock; p98l: Ullstein Bild/Getty Images; p98r: Peter Kotoff/Shutterstock; p99t: Greg Williams/Getty Images Entertainment/Getty Images; p99b: United Archives GmbH / Alamy Stock Photo; p103: Ociacia/Shutterstock; p104: Nawa Yantha/Shutterstock; p105: gor.stevanovic/Shutterstock; p107: diversepixel/Shutterstock; p112: NASA/Troy Cryder; p114: Triff/Shutterstock; p114l: Daimond Shutter/Shutterstock; p114r: © Sandro Vannini/Corbis/Image Library; p115: Michal Ninger/Shutterstock; p116: Radiokafka/Shutterstock; p118: Radiokafka/Shutterstock; p119: ImagesBazaar/Getty Images; p120: Viacheslav Lopatin/Shutterstock; p122: Pavel Ilyukhin/Shutterstock; p124: arfabita/Shutterstock; p125: symbiot/Shutterstock; p128: Preto Perola/Shutterstock; p129: graphixmania/Shutterstock; p130: Mykola Mazuryk/Shutterstock; p130l: Silvia Jansen/E+/Getty Images; p130r: Graeme Dawes/Shutterstock; p131t: Dmytro Balkhovitin/Shutterstock; p131b: Incredible Arctic/Shutterstock; p134: SCOTTCHAN/Shutterstock; p135: Lester Balajadia/Shutterstock; p137: mountainpix/Shutterstock; p138: Cameron Strathdee/iStock; p139: FloridaStock/Shutterstock; p142: Pigprox/Shutterstock; p144: Zacarias Pereira da Mata/Shutterstock.

Artwork by OUP and Six Red Marbles.

Anton Chekhov: extract from Act 3, 'Uncle Vanya' from Anton Chekhov: Five Plays (Oxford World Classics, OUP, 1980), reprinted by permission of Oxford University Press.

Philip Gross: extracts from The Lastling (OUP, 2003), copyright © Philip Gross 2003, reprinted by permission of Oxford University Press.

David Harmer: 'My Mum Put Me on the Transfer List', copyright © David Harmer 1998, first published in They Think It's All Over edited by David Orme (Macmillan Children's Books, 1998) reprinted by permission of the author.

*Robert Penn: extract from It's All About the Bike: The Pursuit of Happiness on Two Wheels (Penguin Particular, 2010), copyright © Robert Penn 2010, reprinted by permission of Penguin Books Ltd.

Robert Swindells: extract from In the Nick of Time (Corgi Children's, 2007), reprinted by permission of The Random House Group Ltd

Although we have made every effort to trace and contact all copyright holders before publication this has not been possible in all cases. If notified, the publisher will rectify any errors or omissions at the earliest opportunity.

Contents

Introduction to Student Book 7

Welcome to Oxford's **Complete English for Cambridge Secondary 1 Student Book**. This book and the student workbook will support you and your teacher as you engage with Stage 7 of the Cambridge curriculum framework.

It aims to encourage you in becoming:

- **Confident** in your English skills and your ability to express yourself
- **Responsible** for your own learning and responsive to and respectful of others
- **Reflective** as a learner so that you can be a life-long learner – not just in school now
- **Innovative** and ready for new challenges as a global citizen
- **Engaged** in both academic and social situations.

Student book and Workbook

There are some great features in your Stage 7 book. Here's an explanation of how they work.

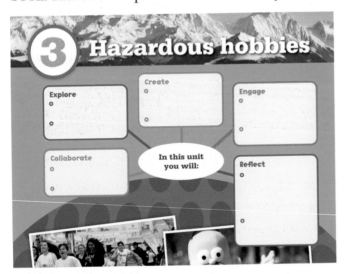

At the start of every unit, you'll see this diagram above. It gives you a quick summary of what the unit will be about and what kind of activities you'll engage with.

Each unit has a global theme. You'll explore science, technology, the universe and space in Unit 7, *Sizzling science*. Journey across the world in the company of the great adventurer Phileas Fogg in *Joyous journeys* and find out about food facts and persuasive opinions in *Food for thought*.

Through the *Thinking time* and *Speaking and listening* features you get the chance to express what you already know about a theme or topic, think critically and find out more from your classmates whilst exploring new ideas.

 Reading

Every day, each of us reads all kinds of texts, for example; novels, recipes, newspapers, blogs, bicycle repair manuals, cartoons, school reports! We read from books, phones, computers, tablets, food packaging and bus timetables. In this Stage 7 book you'll encounter all kinds of texts to enhance your reading experience. From Charlotte's weird time-slip in the Sci-Fi fiction extract 'In the Nick of Time' to stormy poems in *Nurturing nature*, unit 9 and a drama playscript, you'll be discovering both the literal and literary world around you. Comprehension tasks help you to show that you understand explicit and implicit meaning and lead from information retrieval to generating new ideas and material.

As you read, use the Word Clouds that appear alongside on the same pages to learn new vocabulary, explore meanings and usage in context. The Glossary will help you with words or phrases that you may not find in a dictionary because they are uncommon, colloquial or technical phrases.

 ## Vocabulary

Learning new words and perhaps more importantly, learning exactly how they should be used is a key element of this series of books. There are lots of *word building* exercises for you to extend and enhance your vocabulary. Don't expect to know all the words you encounter, – it's our aim to help you build up your vocabulary.

 ## Listening

Throughout every unit there are listening tasks, where the transcript or 'text' of what you hear does not appear printed in your book. Sometimes, your teacher may provide you with the transcript of the audio recording to support you. You will hear a radio news report about a fire at a fireworks factory, a conversation between 12-year-old Ghada and her grandparents, a speech by an author talking about how he writes suspense fiction. As you listen, you will be practising your skills of listening to locate details, listening to understand the gist of what is being said, and listening to make inferences… trying to work out what people really mean!

Language development

Developing your language is more than just learning grammar! It gives your spoken and written 'language muscles' the chance to grow strong. Then you'll be able to express yourself clearly, accurately and impressively! The language awareness and development activities in this Stage 7 book will improve your grammar, spelling and punctuation. Uncover what contractions, connotations and clichés really mean and how using them or *not* using them empowers your language.

 ## Writing

Every unit has a writer's workshop where you will learn skills of writing for different purposes linked to some of the texts you have read in the unit. In Stage 7 you will write a dramatic suspense narrative, an article for a local newspaper, create your own sports kenning and travel into your family's past to construct a biography of one of your grandparents. With step by step guidance, you will develop the structure and organize your ideas using a range of sentences and presentations to become a powerful, engaging and accurate writer.

Reflecting and checking progress

Progress check ✔

Reflecting on your learning

Being a responsible learner means discovering your progress and planning what you need to do to improve and move forward. Workbook 7 enables you to practise and expand on what you've been doing in lessons independently or for homework.

Each unit ends with a quick, fun quiz as a 'progress check' and a personal reflection so that you can understand your own personal development in English.

In this unit you will:

Explore
- features of successful suspense writing
- different scenarios that create suspense

Create
- your own introductory paragraphs of a suspense story
- your own examples of cliff-hangers, dilemmas and other features of the suspense genre

Engage
- with the macaque monkeys of Gibraltar
- with the life of a Barbadian author

Collaborate
- to explore why horror is so popular a genre
- to explore how the combined use of humour and horror can be effective

Reflect
- on the importance of using different types of sentence in your writing
- on how writers create suspense in their stories

Not everything scary is huge!

I love stories where I'm always on the edge of my seat and maybe a little scared too.

It's the suspense that is best; once you see the scary monsters they're nothing to be afraid of.

Evil, ugly creatures aren't frightening but spiders terrify me.

Thinking time

Myths and legends appear in different cultures. Many of these stories involve horror and suspense.

1. Do you prefer reading scary stories or watching scary movies?
2. Do you agree that what the mind imagines is more terrifying than what the eyes see?
3. Why are stories involving horror and suspense so popular all over the world?

Speaking and listening – Things that frighten people

Answer these questions.

1. Make a list of all the scary things you can think of.
2. Share your list with a partner. Do you have anything in common?
3. Compile a combined list of the ten scariest things in rank order.
4. Write a definition for the word *horror*.

Creating suspense – the power of suggestion

Suspense suggests a feeling of being anxious or uncertain about what is about to happen next. Many writers use suspense as a device for creating tension within their texts.

Read the following passage and draw the creature as you imagine it.

It lurked in the shadows carefully hidden, silently watching and waiting to pounce. A creature so old and mystical that no human had ever set eyes on its terrifying features until now! Slowly, so slowly, it shifted its enormous bulk and began to move, metre by ponderous metre, towards the unsuspecting crowd.

3

Clinging to the edge

Paris is part of an expedition to the Himalayas to find the legendary yeti. She is helped by her friend Tahr and Geng-sun, the creature she was hunting.

1 The rope ladder went **taut**, and after a moment there was a little hissing in the air, and the end of the spare rope **snaked** back down. Tahr caught it and gave it a firm tug. "There," he said, as if this was a plan they'd already discussed. "We tie this round

5 you. . . so. Then she can hold you if. . ." He stopped. Just the word *fall* might be too much for her.

Easy. All she had to do was. . . trust the **yeh-teh**. With her life.

Tahr had **looped** the rope around her, more than once, just in case, and three or four extra knots at the end to be sure. "Now,"

10 he said gently. "You climb."

"Only if. . . if you climb too. If you. . . talk to me."

"Talk?" Tahr said. "About what?"

"Anything. Please!" said Paris. "I just need to know you're there."

Twice she nearly **blacked out** – she almost wished that she

15 could – and she found herself **clamped** to the ladder, her arms through the rungs and **hugging** it with all her strength. Eyes shut, she felt the rung against her cheek and it was all right, it would be all right as long as she could stay right here and never move again. Except her **calf muscles** were starting to **ache** and

20 tremble. But when she tried to shift her weight at all, the rope ladder swung away and she **froze** and **clung** again.

From *The **Lastling*** by Philip Gross

Word cloud

ache	hugging
clamped	looped
clung	snaked
froze	taut

Understanding

Answer the following questions.

1. How does Tahr try to help Paris to make the climb?

2. Paris has to trust the 'yeh-teh' to keep her safe but why might this be a problem for her?

3. In the first paragraph how do you know that Paris is frightened by the climb?

4. How is the author successful in creating suspense in the last paragraph of the extract?

Glossary

Lastling the author's term for the last of its kind

yeh-teh yeti, a legendary creature of the Himalayas

blacked out became unconscious

calf muscles the muscles in the lower leg area

Verbs

Every sentence contains at least one verb. Verbs are used to describe a state, an action or a feeling. They are sometimes called 'doing' words.

When trying to create suspense, a writer will describe *exactly* the way a character feels or moves, using a variety of verbs to build the image. **Example**:

> Except her calf muscles were starting to ache and tremble.

The verb *tremble* is used to show how much she is suffering. Trembling suggests fear of losing her footing and falling, so its use builds suspense.

"Hmm, I need a really good verb here."

Developing your language – using verbs to create suspense

Answer these questions.

1. Write an alternative verb that creates more suspense than those in bold below.

   a The climber was **worried** the avalanche would bury him.

   b "Run for your life!" **said** the lifeguard when he saw the shark.

   c "**Hit** the alarm as hard as you can or it won't work."

2. Write as many alternatives as you can for these verbs:

   talk   move   said

 # Word builder

Answer the following questions.

1. Look at the words in the Word cloud. Most are different forms of verbs.

   a *Taut* is not a verb. What kind of word is it?

   b Why is *taut* more effective than using *stretched*?

2. How is the use of *froze* instead of *stopped* and *clung* instead of *held* so effective in explaining Paris' fear? How does it relate to the use of *clamped* and *hugging*?

3. How does *looped* make the image clearer than if the writer has used *tied* in the phrase "Tahr *tied* the rope around her"?

Types of sentence

A sentence is a group of words containing a subject, a verb and sometimes an object that makes complete sense on its own. **Example**:

I am going to the cinema.

Here, the subject is *I* and the verb is *am going* – the sentence is a complete idea. This is called a main clause, or an independent clause.

A **simple sentence** usually consists of one main (independent) clause. **Example**:

The teenager was really scared of theme parks.

Here, the subject is the *teenager* and the verb is *scared*.

A **compound sentence** contains two or more main (independent) clauses that may be joined using a conjunction.

Example:

I am going to the cinema but I don't want to see a scary film.

We can use simple sentences to:

state one idea clearly:
Rollercoasters scare me.

make important points:
I don't like being thrown around.

ask questions:
Do you like theme parks?

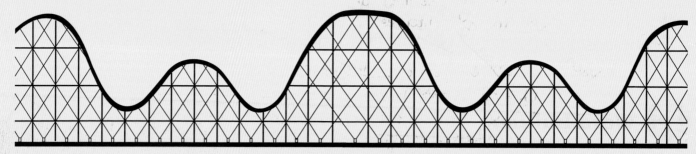

Two simple sentences join together to make a compound sentence.

My name is Ali.

and

I am a huge fan of theme parks.

Using different types of sentence

Remember

Conjunctions are joining words. Examples:

and, as, but, because, or, so

Answer the following questions.

1. Read this simple sentence.

   Tamsin loves rollercoasters.

   a Who is the subject in this sentence?

   b What verb is used?

   c Add four more simple sentences to form a paragraph about Tamsin's love of rollercoasters.

2. Which of these are not simple sentences and why?

   a I become dizzy on rollercoasters.

   b When I came off the rollercoaster, I felt sick because the rollercoaster moved too fast.

   c It is best not to eat before riding a big rollercoaster.

   d I like gentle rides since I don't get scared.

3. Read this sentence.

   I was apprehensive the first time I rode a rollercoaster but I loved the thrill it gave me.

   a Who is the subject in each main clause?

   b Which two verbs are used?

   c What is the conjunction used?

4. Ali has written a blog post about his latest rollercoaster experience but it is all in simple sentences. Rewrite this blog post using conjunctions.

   I went on holiday to Abu Dhabi. I wanted to ride Formula Rossa. The theme park is called Ferrari World. I rode Formula Rossa three times. The ride reaches 150 km/h. It is the fastest in the world. You reach 1.7G of force. You feel like you are in a Formula 1 racing car. This is the best rollercoaster I have ever ridden. The ride is not the most frightening in the world. I want to go back to the park. I can't wait to ride Formula Rossa again.

5. Write your own compound sentence by adding a conjunction and an independent clause to each of these simple sentences.

   a People love to ride fast rollercoasters.

   b The suspense before we start moving is my favourite part.

   c I love being turned upside down.

   d My friend hates rollercoasters.

See Monkey: Fear Monkey

1   I have absolutely no desire to visit the 'apes' den'. I'd rather swim with sharks or wrestle a crocodile but there's no way I'm going to avoid it. My monkey-loving daughter has spoken.

The famous **Barbary apes** of **Gibraltar** are as much a part of
5   the story of Gibraltar as their human neighbours. They have survived two World Wars, countless attempts at invasion and still they **persistently** refuse to surrender.

They are **relentlessly inquisitive** and **permanently** hungry. Any plastic bag is an invitation to explore and feast, even if it means
10 an all-out **assault** on the owner. They are not **averse** to a touch of armed **robbery**: for **relatively** small animals they have huge and **extremely** sharp **incisors**, and they have an expectation that anything they take a fancy to belongs to them. You are advised to stay at least one metre away, not provoke them and, under no
15 circumstances, feed them. The main problem with this advice is that the monkeys **completely** ignore it. Resistance is pointless. Think cute and cuddly then add **psychotic** and **malevolent**.

They frighten me to death! I become a quivering six feet tall jelly at the very thought of a close encounter with these **devious**
20 **thugs** of the animal world.

Word cloud

completely	relatively
extremely	relentlessly
permanently	robbery
persistently	

Glossary

assault attack

averse opposed to

Barbary apes a species of monkey found in Gibraltar

devious thug clever but violent person

fair game an informal term for an acceptable target

Gibraltar a territory situated at the end of the Iberian Peninsula in Southern Europe

incisors pointed teeth for biting

inquisitive curious

malevolent evil

psychotic crazy

Understanding

Answer the following questions.

1. Why does the writer have to visit the 'apes' den'?
2. How does the writer make the monkeys sound dangerous?
3. How might someone who likes monkeys make the writer's negative comments more positive?

 ## Talking monkeys

Discuss these questions with a partner.

1. How does the writer create humour in the extract?
2. Does using humour make the monkeys less frightening?

Adverb

An adverb gives information about a verb or adjective.

Example:

> We tried to run quickly to escape the situation.

The adverb *quickly* suggests how they ran.

Many adverbs end in –*ly*. An adverb can also answer questions, for example, "How?"

Developing your language – adverbs

Find the adverb in each of these examples.

1. We met frequently before the voyage to plan our trip.

2. I asked hesitantly if I had done something wrong.

3. No one knew what the morning would bring but fearlessly we walked on anyway.

 ## Word builder

Answer the following questions.

1. Look at the words in the Word cloud.

   a Find the word that is not an adverb.

   b What kind of word is it?

   c How did you know by just looking that it wasn't an adverb?

2. *Permanently*, *persistently* and *relentlessly* are all adverbs that were adjectives before the –*ly* ending was added. Write a sentence for each one, using it as an adjective.

3. Some words can appear in different forms in different contexts. *Extremely* and *relatively* are examples. If you drop the –*ly* ending, both can be adjectives but they can also be nouns. Write a sentence for each one, using it as a noun.

4. Without the –*ly* ending, *completely* becomes an adjective but can also be a verb. Write a sentence to show this.

5. Can you think of any other adjectives that become adverbs when –*ly* is added as an ending?

Remember

An adjective is word that describes a noun (somebody or something).

Example:

The **clever** monkeys steal things.

Complex sentences

A **complex sentence** contains one main (independent) clause and one or more subordinate (dependent) clauses.
Example:

I am really scared of monkeys: they move so fast and they bite.

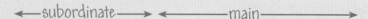
←————main————→ ←subordinate→ ←subordinate→

Here, the main clause tells you the subject is afraid of monkeys and the subordinate clauses tell you the monkeys are quick and dangerous.

Complex sentences are used when more information is required about the subject of the sentence.

The main clause can also appear after the subordinate clause, separated by a comma. **Example**:

When it was younger, the ogre was afraid of humans.

←——subordinate——→ ←————main————→

The *ogre* is the subject and *was* is the verb. The main idea is that the ogre was afraid. The subordinate idea tells you when this happened.

Can I join you please?

Main man

Subordinate

Using complex sentences

Answer these questions.

1. Identify the main and subordinate clauses in these sentences.

   a She still loved him after the accident in the laboratory.

   b He had to save his friend because she was afraid of heights.

   c Before I became a horror writer, I never watched anything except comedies.

2. Add a suitable subordinate clause to each of these main clauses.

   a The thrill of the chase excited him.

   b Dangling from the edge of the cliff didn't worry him.

   c Don't ask me why I am so afraid.

Remember

A main (independent) clause can be used on its own but a subordinate (dependent) clause must be attached to a main clause for it to make sense.

Key concept

Subordinating conjunctions

A **subordinating conjunction** joins the subordinate clause to the main clause. It is always positioned at the beginning of the subordinate clause. **Examples**:

After they enjoyed a fine dinner, the host narrated an excellent spine-chilling tale.

The host narrated an excellent spine-chilling tale *after* they enjoyed a fine dinner.

In both cases, *after* is the word that joins the two clauses, irrespective of which is written first. It tells you when the tale was told.

Using subordinating conjunctions

Answer the following questions.

1. Complete these complex sentences using the most appropriate conjunction in each case.

  a _____ I've seen *King Kong* many times, I'd like to see it again.

    Whenever   Because   Even though

  b _____ I watch a horror movie, I always keep my eyes partially closed.

    If   As   Since

  c This is a tense movie _____ the acting is so realistic.

    whereas   because   until

  d I've read thrillers _____ I was 10 years old.

    when   although   since

2. Change the conjunctions used in these sentences to improve them.

  a But I went to the comic store, I read my copy of *Suspense*.

  b My all-time favourite character is the werewolf if I like the other characters also.

  c I read three thrillers a week whereas I have the time.

3. Write two paragraphs about your favourite book or movie. Use at least three complex sentences in each paragraph.

 # The Key to Writing Suspense

An author has just been given an award. Listen to his account of becoming a writer, and what he thinks are the most important features of writing suspense.

Understanding

Answer these questions.

1. On what island was the author born?

2. Give the two meanings of the word *Bajan*. Use your dictionary to help you.

3. Do you agree that the author was lucky in his success?

4. Which do you think is the most important tip the author gave about the successful writing of suspense?

5. How difficult do you think it would be to become a best-selling author?

 # Describing Barbados

Use the author's speech to imagine what Barbados may be like.

Carry out research on Barbados and discuss your findings.

> **Key concept**
>
> ### Ellipses
>
> An ellipsis is a series of three dots used to show an omission from written text. It can be used in writing to create suspense. **Example:**
>
> > I stood at the doorway to the strange old house… I don't remember entering… the hallway reeked of something I couldn't quite place.

Using ellipsis

Use ellipses in the following piece of writing.

Imagine you are in the house and you walk into the kitchen. Write a paragraph describing what you see and include ellipses in several places.

Glossary

Barbadians natives of Barbados

Barbados a Caribbean island

climax the most important part of a story or event

Daily Nation a Barbadian newspaper

dilemma a major problem

Washington, D.C. capital city of USA

Hyphens

Hyphens join two or more words to show that they have a combined meaning, creating compound nouns, adjectives or verbs, e.g. *fire-fighter, part-time, test-drive*. These words are always hyphenated.

Other words are only hyphenated to show that they are linked in the grammar of a sentence. This helps to avoid ambiguity. **Example**:

> My grandmother owns a little-used car.

Grandmother's little-used car

Developing your language – hyphenated words

Answer these questions.

1. Which of the words from this list are fixed compounds (i.e. they always have to be hyphenated) and which are not? Use a dictionary to help you.

fast-paced	fifty-fifty	sub-plot	long-range
open-handed	short-sighted	long-term	re-edit

2. Explain the difference in meaning of these two sentences and why a hyphen is necessary in the second example.

    The writer *resigned* from his contract.
    The writer *re-signed* to extend his contract.

 Word builder

Use the words in the Word cloud to complete the following.

1. A *cliff-hanger* is not someone hanging from a cliff but a literary device. What does the term mean and how appropriate a name do you think it is?

2. *Half-hearted and murder-suspense* are adjectives. What nouns do they describe and how effective are they in expressing the author's ideas?

3. *Sugar cane* does not require a hyphen but the writer wants to create a play on words in the title of his new book.

    a   By making it 'Sugar-cane Frame' what happens to the rhythm?

    b   Do you think this is an effective use of a hyphen?

4. Write three other phrases that require hyphens to avoid confusion.

 # Writing suspense – planning a beginning

You are going to plan and write the first two paragraphs of a suspense story. Use the guidance provided to help you.

 # Planning meeting

Discuss the advice the author gave for successful suspense writing. What are you going to write about? How does his advice fit in?

Planning your paragraphs

You want to grab the reader's attention immediately so your opening paragraphs have to be fast-paced, eventful, and leave the reader wanting to find out more.

Planning the introduction:

- What location will you use? Choose a familiar setting so you can add detail from memory.
- Who is the main character? Think about name, gender, age, personality.
- Will you use first or third person narrative?
- What major crisis will your character face?
- What dilemma must be overcome?
- What is the time pressure?

The opening paragraph:

Remember to introduce

- your main character
- the location
- the crisis
- the time pressure.

The second paragraph:

- the dilemma and its link to the story
- more details about the character, location, and time pressure
- the cliff-hanger.

Elements of suspense

Try to include most of these elements in your writing to provide an explosive start to the story.

Use the graphic as a checklist for your story.

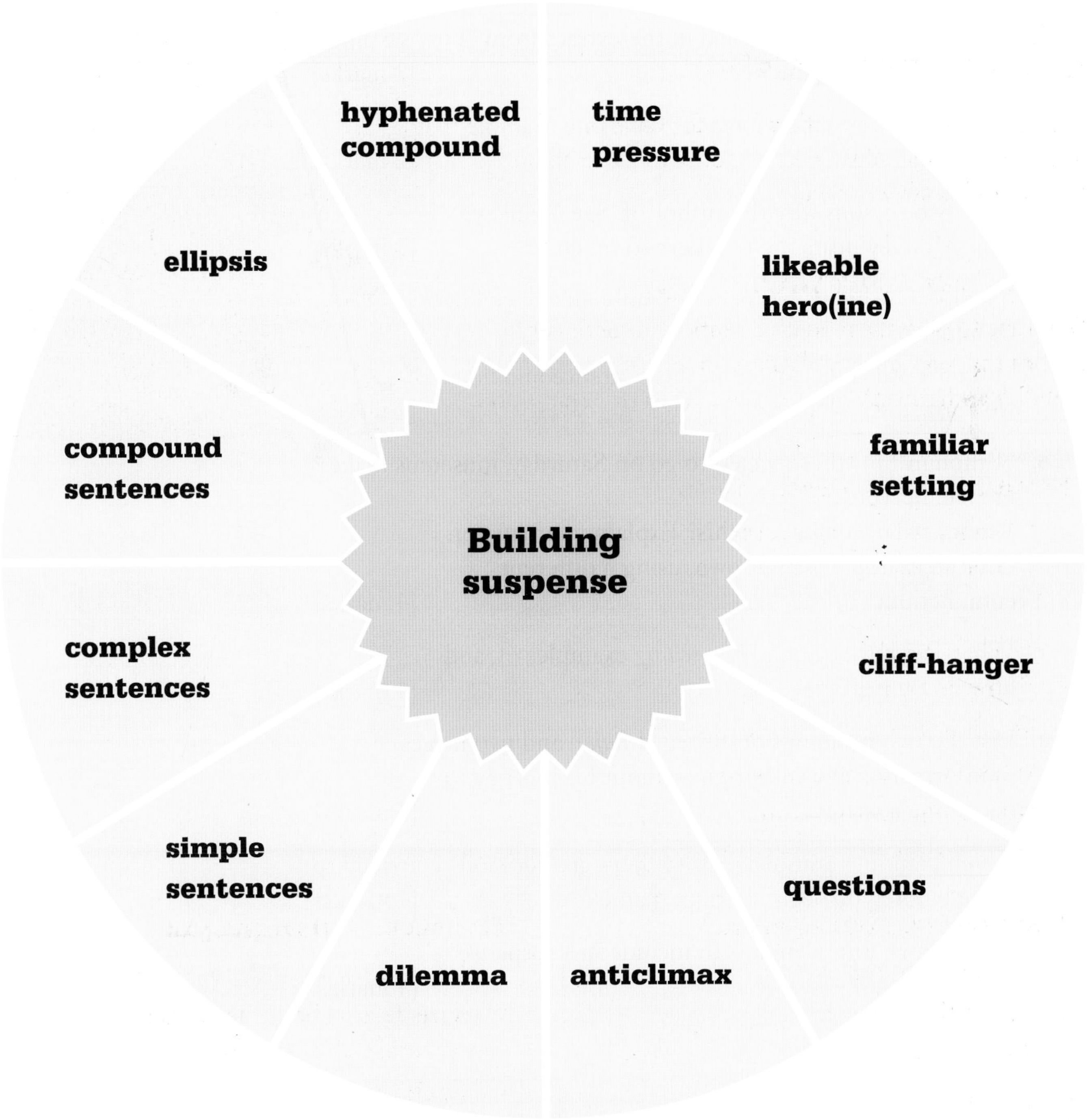

Building suspense

- hyphenated compound
- time pressure
- ellipsis
- likeable hero(ine)
- compound sentences
- familiar setting
- complex sentences
- cliff-hanger
- simple sentences
- questions
- dilemma
- anticlimax

Progress check

1. 'It lurked in the shadows carefully hidden, silently watching and waiting to pounce.'

   Give two reasons why this opening creates suspense.   [2 marks]

2. Why was Paris so frightened in the extract from 'The Lastling' and who tried to calm her?   [2 marks]

3. What is a compound sentence? Give one example that creates suspense.   [2 marks]

4. Give two reasons why the author of 'See Monkey: Fear Monkey' fears the monkeys so much.   [2 marks]

5. 'Haunted by his experiences, fearfully he glanced over his shoulder.'

   Which word is the adverb in this sentence and how do we know this?   [2 marks]

6. 'Although I'm still expected to go on Saturday, museums make me feel nervous.'
   What kind of sentence is this? Explain your answer.
   Give an example of your own, using a different conjunction.   [4 marks]

7. What are *cross-breed* and *best-selling* examples of, and how do they differ?   [4 marks]

8. List the two meanings of the word *Bajan* and two pieces of information the author gives about his journey to becoming a writer.   [4 marks]

9. When planning a suspense story there are decisions you need to make before you begin writing. Name four of these.   [4 marks]

10. Write down four elements to include in a suspense story.   [4 marks]

Reflecting on your learning – climbing the 'peak of success'

I've reached the summit and feel really confident – I wrote a successful suspense story introduction using lots of the elements

I'm almost there; just one more push needed – I included most of the elements of a successful suspense story in my introductory paragraphs

I'm halfway up but I've needed help to climb – I understood the elements but couldn't use many in my paragraphs

Base-camp: I'm still practising and need more help – I found writing the paragraphs a challenge

The foothills: I've made a start, but it looks a long way up – I needed more help with the paragraphs

Action plan

Thinking about how high you've climbed up the 'Peak of success', answer the following:

?

Did I struggle with any of the writing skills?

What can I do better to climb higher?

How am I going to do this?

2 Manic media

In this unit you will:

Explore
- a South American seaside town
- the scene at a fireworks factory

Create
- a diary entry by a waiter in a restaurant
- a news report about a local event

Engage
- with letters written to express differing views
- with the presentation of radio news

Collaborate
- to design the front page of a newspaper
- to resolve an argument

Reflect
- on how a newspaper office is organised
- on how life in a small town is upset by new developments

Turn off the news! It's trouble, trouble, trouble!

News is boring. I prefer to watch the adverts!

Whatever they say, the news is always biased one way or another. They decide what you are going to be told, so you can't make up your own mind.

Thinking time

Think about your experience of reading, watching, and listening to the news.

1. Do you think that the news is nothing but 'trouble, trouble, trouble'?

2. What do you think 'boring' means, and why may people say that news is 'boring'?

3. What is meant by news being 'biased'? How do you think it can be biased? Is the quotation fair?

Editor-in-chief: the boss of the newspaper team, responsible for all important decisions

Layout of newspaper articles

Each newspaper story has a **headline**, which is bigger than the main (body) text. Its words are meant to attract attention. Newspaper stories appear in **columns** and the design of the page is called the **layout**. Pictures are given **captions**.

News editor: decides which stories are the most important and how much room each one has

Speaking and listening

In groups, based on the roles of the newspaper team, decide what the front page of your newspaper will cover tomorrow. You have a choice of stories:

- an athlete wins a gold medal at an international event
- the government introduces new taxes
- a heat wave may continue for another month.

You only have room for one photograph, but it can be quite large.

You must decide on the following:

- which story or stories will go on the front page tomorrow
- what you want the reporter to write in the story and what headline you might use to grab readers' attention
- what photograph you will use to illustrate the story and why.

Picture editor: chooses photographs that give the right message and decides on their size

Reporter: goes out to find information and writes the story

Your newspaper team

Front page story

Tempers tested at hotel development meeting

1   by our regional correspondent Christina Acosta
**Angry residents hurled insults at each other
yesterday at a meeting in the remote seaside
town of Bellavista.**

5   Few tourists come to this **peaceful** harbour that
has no gas station and only one run-down café.
The residents prize the **golden** beaches and
sparkling sea.

Now a developer plans to build a 100-bedroom
10   hotel and an eco-friendly theme park here.

At yesterday's meeting the mayor, Councillor
Sanchez, spoke in favour of the development
and was vociferously supported by residents
anxious to profit from visitors to Bellavista.

15   "Look to the future," he said. "Our town is a
backwater. Some of our houses are dilapidated.
We are dying a slow death."
Señora Alonso, a highly respected resident,
abruptly interrupted. She warned that Bellavista's

tranquil atmosphere and **picturesque** beauty 20
were in terrible danger as the plans were more
extensive than Councillor Sanchez claimed. She
was sure people would vote against them. Wild
applause followed. Residents accused the mayor
of plotting behind their backs. He could not keep 25
order and had to leave.

Understanding

Answer the following questions.

1. Why is the first sentence in bold? What information does
   this sentence give?

2. Why do you think few tourists come to Bellavista?

3. What details about the town has the reporter included, and
   why do you think they are important?

4. Re-read the report. Do you think it is biased? Explain your
   answer.

Word cloud

golden   sparkling

peaceful   tranquil

picturesque

Glossary

backwater away from the
busy town life

hurled insults exchanged
angry words

rundown in bad condition

Developing your language – creating images

The report uses the words *backwater*, *dilapidated*, and *rundown* to describe Bellavista.

What image does this create?

You can create an image by choosing adjectives carefully. For example, you could describe the seafront at Bellavista as *clean*. It would be much better to say *spotless* though. Describing the walkways as *gleaming* or *glistening* would build up an effective image.

 **Looking closely**

The words *dilapidated*, *interrupted*, and *vociferously* come from Latin. Originally, *lapid* came from a word meaning stone, *rupt* meaning broken and *voc* meaning voice.

 Word builder

Answer the following questions.

1. Look at the words in the Word cloud.

   a Why is *peaceful* better than *little* harbour?

   b Why is *sandy* better than *yellow* beaches?

   c Why is *sparkling* better than *clean* seawater?

2. Find some powerful adjectives to describe these things you would find at the seaside:

   a cliffs   **b** fish   **c** a fishing boat.

3. Improve the message on the postcard by changing the adjectives into more interesting ones.

   I had a **good** holiday near Bellavista. The weather was **nice**. The hotel had a **big** swimming pool and I enjoyed **pleasant** meals.

> **Remember**
>
> An adjective is a describing word. It is often used in front of a noun.

Key concept

Adjectives

Choose strong adjectives to describe things when you write and avoid words such as *nice, good, boring* and *OK*. This will give a clear image, for example of a place or a person and your feelings about them. You can use your words to persuade a reader to agree with you.

Direct and indirect speech

Direct speech shows what a person actually says. **Example:**

"Good evening, fellow residents," said the mayor.

To punctuate direct speech, you should:

- open speech marks when someone begins to speak
- close speech marks when this person stops speaking
- use a capital letter for the first word someone says
- add punctuation before closing speech marks
- start a new line when a new person speaks.

Using direct speech

Answer the following questions.

1. Correct the following direct speech by adding punctuation.

   Look to the future he said Our town is a backwater We are dying a slow death

2. Change the following sentences into direct speech, adding correct punctuation.

   a i think the hotel will dwarf the whole town said one speaker

   b i think said a shopkeeper thoughtfully that this development will increase my profits

   c aren't you being selfish asked a little old lady well perhaps answered the shopkeeper but isn't my future important too

Indirect (reported) speech describes what a person says without using their actual words. **Example:**

Señora Alonso said that she was extremely angry with the mayor's plans.

To change direct to indirect speech, you should:

- remove speech marks
- change verbs from present to past tense
- change pronouns to reflect the person speaking (so *I* become *he* or *she*).
- Newspaper stories vary their reports by using a mixture of direct and indirect speech.

Using indirect speech

Change these examples of direct speech into indirect speech.

1. "The mayor is looking very worried," said Señora Alonso.

2. "I am tired of these people who keep on shouting at me," said the mayor. "I am only doing my best for this town."

3. "I wonder what will happen," said the reporter. "I have never been to such an angry meeting. There is a lot of resentment there."

 ## Converting between types of speech

In pairs, say something and ask your partner to say it back to you in indirect speech.

Here is my opinion

Use the following letters to help you decide which side to support in the controversial issue surrounding Bellavista. (Beware of bias in these letters!)

Letters to the Editor

Mayor's disgraceful behaviour

Sir,

Our mayor's behaviour has **horrified** our desperate residents. We were only made aware of his underhand tactics at the beginning of Wednesday's disgraceful meeting.

The truth of the matter is that this **gigantic** hotel and the so-called eco-theme park will bring floods of visitors to our town. Their cars and buses will **choke** our narrow streets. The result will be **chaos**! I believe that one hotel will lead to other **monstrosities** springing up in every little corner of our beloved Bellavista. What a terrible **tragedy**!

Let us all campaign to defeat this dangerous and destructive proposal.

Maria Alonso

Getting the facts right

Sir,

As a recent resident of Bellavista, I can naturally understand the controversy caused by the proposal to build a hotel. Those who oppose it should carefully consider the facts.

This hotel will definitely be built outside the town and cars will, as at present, be absolutely banned from the centre. The eco-theme park is educational and will be strictly targeted at hard-working, well-behaved children. Finally, this developer has promised to create 120 jobs for local people. A similar development in the town where I used to live has increased the revenues of local shops five-fold.

The peace and prosperity of our town seem safely protected.

José Moreno

Understanding

Answer these questions.

1. Using two headings, 'Facts' and 'Opinions', list the facts and opinions you can find in the letters.

2. Which opinions could be proved right and which are probably wrong?

3. Are the facts enough to persuade you which side to support? Explain your answer.

Word cloud

chaos	horrified
choke	monstrosities
gigantic	tragedy
controversy	

Hyperbole

Hyperbole (pronounced *hy–per–bo–lee*) is a deliberate exaggeration that is not meant to be taken literally.

Example:

Señora Alonso says the development will bring 'floods of visitors' to the town but she doesn't really mean that the people are like a river bursting its banks.

Remember

A fact is something that is true or has happened. An opinion is what you think about it.

Developing your language – hyperbole

Answer the following questions.

1. *Choke*. Choking is a very dangerous condition that can stop someone from breathing properly by completely or partially blocking their throat. Why is it a good word to describe what happens when cars and buses fill narrow streets?

2. *Gigantic*. Could a giant really live in this hotel? Suggest a more realistic word to describe the size of the hotel.

3. *Horrified*. Were the residents really struck with horror? Suggest a more accurate description of how they felt.

4. *Monstrosities*. What did the Señora really mean when she linked hotels with monsters?

5. *Tragedy*. Tragedies are Greek plays in which the characters meet sad deaths. A tragedy is also an event causing great suffering and distress. Suggest a more neutral word for Señora Alonso to use here.

 ## Looking closely

Hyperbole comes from a Greek word, *hyper*, that means 'too or very much'. If you don't sit still, someone might call you *hyperactive*.

Arguing the issue

Imagine you and your friend have lived all your lives in Bellavista. You support the development and your friend does not. List the main points each of you would make to argue your case before carrying out a discussion on this topic. Remember to give facts and opinions that would be used to support each view and use exaggerated language.

Adverbs

Adverbs give added meaning to the verbs in the sentences you write.

A **verb** tells you something that is done, for example, *said*. An adverb describes how a verb is done, for example, *loudly*.

Adverbs are generally formed by adding *–ly* to adjectives.
Examples:

   careful → carefully

   definite → definitely

However, for words already ending in *–y*, change the *y* to an *i*.
Example:

   hungry → hungrily

Words ending in *–ble* should also have their endings changed.
Example:

   horrible → horribly

Using and spelling adverbs

Answer the following questions.

1. Make a list of all the adverbs José Moreno uses in his letter and, next to each one, write the adjective it comes from.

2. Write adverbs made from:

   a *powerful, joyful, thoughtful*

   b *total, fatal, local*

   c *immediate, complete, rare*

   d *greasy, messy, pretty.*

   e *terrible, comfortable, sensible.*

A game with adverbs

Here's a game based on adverbs. Tell someone to walk slowly, hastily, then clumsily, acting out the adverb. Then change the adverb, walk like that, and ask others guess the word. Do the same with *talk*, *smile*, or *sit*.

Using adverbial phrases

You can use phrases to work in the same way as single-word adverbs. **Examples:**

The waiter made his way *across the restaurant.*

He greeted the family *with a friendly smile.*

Single-word adverbs and adverbial phrases can also be used in the same sentence. **Examples:**

The waiter returned *apologetically without the food.*

He said they would have to wait *patiently for a while.*

When the food *finally* arrived *after a long wait,* the breathless waiter *dramatically tripped over a table leg.*

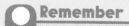

Remember

A phrase is a group of words without a verb.

Answer the questions below.

1. Which prepositions are used to link the phrases in each of the examples?

2. Copy and complete the following using adverbial phrases.

   The waiter wrote the diners' orders _____.

   Federico, the son, looked forward to his fish meal _____.

   Unfortunately, the family had to wait _____.

3. Which of the phrases in the examples tell you how, how long, and where?

4. Write the story as an entry in the waiter's diary.

   Use some of the adverbs and language from the examples, but use some of your own.

   Include how you felt about your difficult day.

Remember

A **preposition** is a word that shows how things are connected like place (on, in), direction (over, across) or time (after, during).

 # Firework inferno!

Listen to the news from Radio Uno about a fire at a local fireworks factory. You will hear two new readers, a reporter at the scene, and the chief fire officer.

Understanding

Answer these questions.

1. When did the fire break out?

2. How many people work at the factory and why were they not hurt in the fire?

3. When the news programme was recorded, why was it not yet possible to say how the fire started?

4. What did the police do to ensure that the people who lived near to the factory were safe?

5. Why did Radio Uno need Mercedes Cardoso to report from the scene of the fire? What did she add to what Daniela Ruiz said?

Developing your language – words to fit the occasion

Radio broadcasts need special language to describe unusual events because they cannot show listeners images.

Words in the report were chosen to stand out when you hear them.

Say these words several times:

con – fla – **gra** – tion	py – ro – **tech** – nics
in – **fer** – no	**rain** – bow
kal – **ei** – dos – cope	spec – **tac** – u – lar

When you write, use a selection of long and short words for effect, but make sure you know the meaning of the long words you use.

Answer these questions.

1. Suggest six words you can use to describe fireworks in the sky. Hint: Think about sounds and smells, not just how fireworks appear.

2. Imagine you were at the scene of the fire at the fireworks factory. Email a friend to describe what you saw and heard. Finish by describing what it was like when the fireworks finally stopped.

Word cloud

conflagration
inferno
kaleidoscope
pyrotechnics
rainbow
spectacular

Glossary

breaking news news that is happening at that moment

keep you up to date tell you anything new that happens

 Word builder

Carry out the following activities.

1. Look up the definition for each word in the Word cloud.

2. For the groups of words below, choose the word that gives the strongest and most powerful image. Explain your answer. Example:

daylight   *rainbow*   *sunset*

Daylight is a general type of light, so this is not a word that gives a very strong impression.

A *rainbow* includes seven different colours and stands out well in the sky.

A *sunset* often has brilliant shades of red and orange that cover most of the sky.

You may therefore choose *sunset* or *rainbow*.

a *bonfire, conflagration, blaze*

b *inferno, confusion, storm*

c *lightshow, colours, kaleidoscope*

d *pyrotechnics, show, illuminations*

e *showy, spectacular, sensational*

Writing your own news report

Ever fancied being a reporter? Now's your opportunity!

Write a news report for a local newspaper about something that happened at your school or in your town. Example:

> ## Argument breaks out at 'friendly' football match

> ## School decides to start lessons at 6am

> ## Popular head teacher takes charge of ultra-modern school

Decide who, what, where, when, why, and how.

Who? Who are the important people in your story? Are they like you? How old are they? Are they rich or poor? Are they famous? What is interesting about them?

What? What happened? What part did the important people play? Were they victims? Did they help other people? Did they achieve something? Were they heroes or bystanders?

Where? Exactly where did the event in your story happen?

When? On which day did the event happen? At what time did it happen?

Why? What are the facts about why the event happened?

How? For example, how did someone achieve something, or how did an event build up from a small beginning to something much bigger?

Planning your report

Before you start writing, use a plan like the one on the opposite page to make notes, so that you get the details of your report in the right order, and to ensure you have the correct layout for your newspaper story.

In your report you need to include what people said. You will need direct and indirect speech.

> 💡 **Remember**
>
> Direct speech is when you use speech marks and write down the words that people say. Indirect speech is when you tell the story of what people said.

My newspaper report

What is the headline?

Who? _____
_____

What happened? _____
_____
_____

Where and when? _____
_____

Picture with caption

Describe exactly what happened, why it happened, and use quotations from people who were there.

_____
_____
_____
_____

Say how the event ended.

_____
_____

Think of a headline

Your headline will be in large print so people must be interested in it and want to read your report.

Argument breaks out at 'friendly' football match is interesting because there's a joke about 'friendly'. As it has two words starting with the letter *f*, it is also an example of alliteration.

Make sure your headline stands out so that people will want to read it!

💡 Remember

Alliteration is when you start two or more words with the same letter or sound. **Example:** amazing ant

Progress check ✔

1. Name two different roles in a newspaper team. [2 marks]

2. Give an example of a fact and an example of an opinion. [2 marks]

3. What is a hyperbole and why might someone use it when they write? [2 marks]

4. What are two characteristics of a good headline? [2 marks]

5. Why did Señora Alonso and José Moreno decide to write letters to the newspaper? [2 marks]

6. Make these adjectives into adverbs and give two more examples of adverbs formed in this way.

   a *eternal*

   b *easy*. [4 marks]

7. In Latin, *spectare* means to look at. Identify the four words beginning with *spec* using the following clues:

   a worn on the nose

   b a person who watches an event

   c really wonderful to watch

   d a show or a drama [4 marks]

8. What are four differences between direct and indirect speech? [4 marks]

9. What is bias? Give three examples of how a newspaper might be biased in its reporting. [4 marks]

10. Describe four features that can make a newspaper report attractive to read. [4 marks]

Reflecting on your learning – listening effectively

Choose one of the words in blue beside each picture that describes how you feel about each of the statements about listening skills.

 I can listen for several minutes without distraction.

Usually/Sometimes/Not often

 I can discuss what I have heard with other people.

Usually/Sometimes/Not often

 I can grasp the main idea of what I hear.

Usually/Sometimes/Not often

 I use what I have heard to form my own ideas.

Often/Sometimes/Rarely

 I can summarise a number of details.

Usually/Sometimes/Not often

 I remember what I have heard for some time.

Easily/Partly/With difficulty

After you have thought about the listening skills statements, answer the following:

1. What can I do to be a better listener?

2. How could I put the things I've listed in question 1 into action over the next three weeks?

3. How will I know if I'm a better listener by that time?

3 Hazardous hobbies

In this unit you will:

Explore
- several different types of poetry
- poetry from different cultures and times

Create
- your own imagery using similes and metaphors
- your own poem

Engage
- with the appeal of football in many parts of the world
- with the life of a Japanese mountaineer

Collaborate
- in the oral tradition to exchange ideas
- to plan a kenning

Reflect
- on the popularity of some sports and hobbies in different locations in the present and past
- on how your choice of language affects your audience

> The earliest poems were stories set to rhythm and rhyme to make them easier to recall.

> Poems don't have to tell a story but they do have to have a theme.

> Surely no one writes poetry about sports or hobbies, do they?

Thinking time

Early forms of poetry were passed down through generations by speech. Today, most poems are published in written form.

1. In the photos opposite, what type of event are the competitors taking part in?
2. Why are some of them dressed in costumes?
3. Why were the earliest poems structured so they were easier to remember?
4. Do you agree that poems have to have a theme? Explain your answer.

Speaking and listening

Think of a sporting event or a hobby that interests you. Plan what you will say about it, then tell a partner. Your partner then takes a turn. When you have both spoken, analyse your performances and discuss possible improvements.

Non-narrative poetry

Unlike narrative poems, non-narrative poems do not tell a story and may not involve characters or a plot, but they contain a theme or idea. **Example:**

'The Little Master'
Proud as a peacock strutting his stuff,
Smooth as a river as his shots flow,
To all corners of the ground,
Sachin, our magician,
Weaving his spell once again.

In this tribute to Sachin Tendulkar, the Indian cricketer, the central theme is an appreciation of his batting. He is likened to a magician because he can outperform other players.

Notice that not all poems rhyme but they must have rhythm.

Study the poem and answer these questions.

1. Count the syllables in each line. What is the pattern?
2. What kind of rhythm does this create?
3. How does the poem's rhythm reflect the batsman's skill?
4. Does the poem explains its central theme effectively?

Looking closely

Rhythm is one of the four English words that doesn't include a vowel. The others are *spryly*, *sylph* and *syzgy*.

Non-narrative poetry

The following poem by Virgil, about chariot racers (charioteers), was written in Ancient Rome. It has since been translated from Latin.

The charioteers were mainly slaves, but if successful, they would win enough money to buy their freedom.

Word cloud

a-loft	hast
a-low	hindmost
beheld	thou
charioteers	

'Virgil's Georgics'

1   **Hast thou beheld**, when from the jail they start,
The youthful **charioteers** with beating heart
Rush to the race: and panting scarcely bear,
The extremes of feverish hopes and chilling fear;
5   Stoop to the reins and **lash** with all their force;
The **flying chariot** kindles in the course.
And now **a-low** and now **a-loft** they fly,
As **borne through air** and seem to touch the sky:
No stop no stay; but clouds of sand arise,
10   Spurned and cast backwards on the viewers' eyes:
The **hindmost** blows the foam upon the first:
Such is the love of praise and **honourable thirst**.

Translation by John Dryden

Understanding

Study the extract and answer the following questions.

1. Are the charioteers young or old?

2. The poem suggests the charioteers had mixed feelings during the race. What were these feelings?

3. Explain whether this race is dangerous or not.

4. How does the poet make the race sound exciting? Explain your answer.

5. Why might these particular men be more desperate to win than competitors in other sports?

Glossary

borne through air not touching the ground

flying chariot fast-moving, horse-drawn carriage

honourable thirst desire to win

lash to whip (their horse)

Developing your language – understanding the context

Virgil wrote his poem over 2000 years ago but the extract was translated into English 300 years ago. Some of the words and phrases Virgil used are no longer in common use. We use the term *archaic language* to describe these. **Example:** in this rhyming couplet (pair of lines that rhyme):

'Hast thou beheld, when from the jail they start,
The youthful charioteers with beating heart'

I'm so excited!

The first three words may be difficult to understand but the general idea is about young men from jail. 'Beating heart' suggests that the men are excited or frightened.

Answer these questions about the extract.

1. Write a short description of the events described in the extract.

2. Compare your description with a partner's and discuss similarities and differences.

 Word builder

The words in the Word cloud are examples of archaic language.

1. *A-low* and *a-loft* are used to convey movement, and can be have opposite meanings. What modern-day term would you use instead?

2. What modern word does *hast* resemble? Write a sentence that begins with this word.

3. *Charioteers* ends with – *eers*, which is used today. Example: *engineers* – experts of engines.

   a What does *charioteers* tell you about the chariot drivers?

   b List three other words ending in *–eers* and give their meanings. Use a dictionary to help you.

What is imagery?

Imagery is the process of using words to create a picture in the mind of the reader. Look again at the start of the poem about Tendulkar on page 35:

'Proud as a peacock strutting his stuff,
Smooth as a river as his shots flow'

The poet uses two similes here. The first likens Tendulkar to a peacock proudly displaying its impressive plumage. The second links the cricketer's movement to the flow of a river to emphasise how gracefully he plays.

Key concept

Similes and metaphors

A **simile** is a way of comparing a person or a thing to something else. The words *like* and as are often used.
Example:

> The dancer moved as gracefully as a gazelle.

A **metaphor** describes a person or a thing directly as something else. **Example:**

> 'Sachin, our magician,
> Weaving his spell once again.'

Using similes and metaphors

Answer the following questions.

1. How effective is the image of a gazelle in describing how graceful the dancer was?

2. Write similes to create images of the following hazardous hobbies.

a

'*As* or *like*?'

b

'*As* or *like*?'

c

'*As* or *like*?'

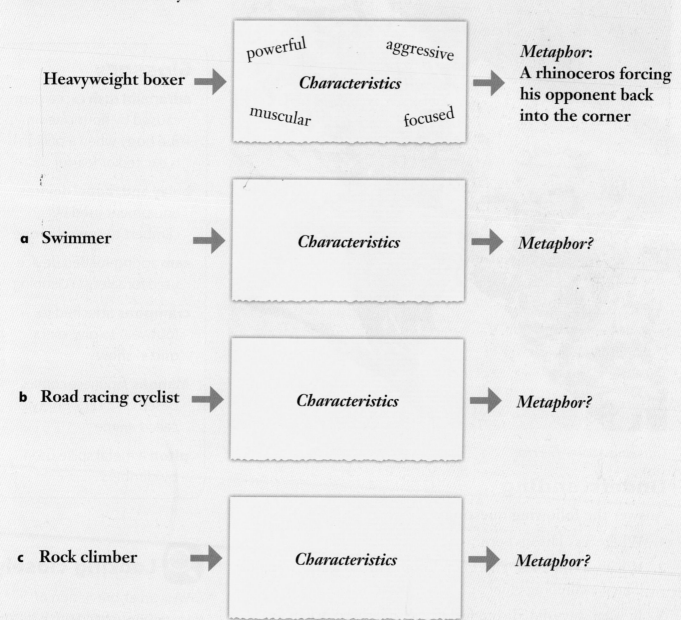

3. Take your three similes from **2**. Change the similes into metaphors.

4. Suggest some characteristics for the following people. Then use the characteristics to help you write a metaphor. The first one has been done for you.

Heavyweight boxer ➡ powerful   aggressive
Characteristics
muscular   focused ➡ *Metaphor*: A rhinoceros forcing his opponent back into the corner

a Swimmer ➡ *Characteristics* ➡ *Metaphor?*

b Road racing cyclist ➡ *Characteristics* ➡ *Metaphor?*

c Rock climber ➡ *Characteristics* ➡ *Metaphor?*

No ordinary pastime

Listen to the interview with world-renowned mountaineer Hiroto Akiyama.

Climbing Mount Everest

Glossary

adrenalin rush excitement caused by hormones in the body when a person is excited or fearful

belay and rappel devices equipment used by climbers to control a rope

cam spring-loaded device used for safety in climbing

crampons attached to footwear to give extra grip in snow

Mangas Japanese comics based on a cartoon style called anime

piton a metal spike used by climbers

Understanding

Answer the following questions.

1. Where was Hiroto born?
2. What was the most important lesson Hiroto learnt when he joined a climbing club?
3. In what ways did Hiroto feel like a 'superhero' when he eventually climbed Mount Fuji?
4. What does Hiroto mean when he says "it isn't in my DNA"?

Looking closely

DNA is an abbreviation of deoxyribonucleic acid. It is the genetic code found in all of our cells.

Homonyms

A **homonym** is a word that has more than one meaning. There are two types of homonym:

1. **Homographs** are words that are spelled the same, but with different meanings. **Example:**

   mould (fungus or shape)

   Sometimes homographs can be pronounced differently. **Example:**

   wind (blowing of air or to twist)

2. **Homophones** are words that sound the same but with different meanings. **Example:**

   currant (dried fruit) and *current* (river flow)

Developing your language – homonyms

Answer the following questions.

1. Write a sentence for each of the photographs showing a meaning for *bow*.

2. Which of the following words are homographs, and which are homonyms?

dessert (after-dinner pudding)   *desert* (to abandon)   *desert* (mass of dry land, often sandy)

 **Word builder**

The words in the Word cloud are homonyms.

1. Write a sentence using *patient* as a noun.
2. Is *patient* a homograph, a homophone, or both?
3. How can *breeds* be used as a noun and not a verb?
4. In the interview *refrain* and *slings* are nouns. Write a sentence for each in their verb forms.
5. Used as a noun *peak* has four different meanings. Write down two of its meanings.
6. *Summit* is a noun with more than one meaning. Use a dictionary to find alternative meanings and write a sentence for each.

Looking closely

The word *homonym* originates from two Greek words: *homos* meaning same and *onyma* meaning name.

Alliteration and assonance

Alliteration and assonance are two literary techniques based on phonic effect – how the sound of the words, phrases, and sentences create a response in the reader.

Alliteration occurs when two or more words close to each other start with the same letter or sound. **Example:**

> Silently and skilfully the Slovakian skier slides smoothly across the soft snow, knowing she will soon finish.

The use of the *s* sound is a specific form of alliteration called **sibilance**.

Assonance occurs when there is a similarity between vowel sounds in two or more words. **Example:**

> The rain in Spain falls mainly on the plain, which makes it a strain to train for the game.

Using alliteration and assonance

Answer the following questions.

1. The commentator of this football game is trying to enthuse the audience with her pre-match comments. List examples of alliteration in her speech.

"Welcome to the Estadio Vicente Calderon, this cauldron of chaos and home to Atlético Madrid. I'm here with forty-four thousand fanatical fans eagerly anticipating this clash of culture against the mercurial magicians of FC Porto. They are the proud Portuguese champions who, no doubt, are plotting and planning to rain on the home team's parade by scoring an away goal in tonight's top-quality Champions League quarter final clash."

2. Write an alliterative paragraph for each of the following occasions.

   a an important hockey match

   b skateboarding practice

   c a trip in a hot air balloon

   d a badminton match.

3. List examples of assonance in the following sentences.

   a She's lean, she's mean, she's a scoring machine!

   b His advantage is not that he towers above everyone but lies in the power with which he shoots.

4. Write a phrase or sentence that includes an example of assonance for:

   a a Formula 1 racing car

   b your favourite sportsperson

   c riding a bicycle up a hill.

5. Consider this rhyming word chain:

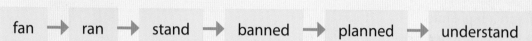

fan → ran → stand → banned → planned → understand

   a Add four more words to the chain that follow the same pattern.

   b Use your word chain to construct a short paragraph that demonstrates your understanding of assonance.

Estadio Vicente Calderon stadium

Poems for fun

Read the following poem.

This poem is unusual because the voice in the title is not the same as the one in the poem itself. Can you spot the literal and implied meanings within the text?

'My Mum Put Me on the Transfer List'

1   On offer:
    one **nippy** striker, ten years old
    has scored seven goals this season
    has **nifty** footwork and a big smile
5   knows how **to dive** in the **penalty box**
    can get filthy and muddy within two minutes
    guaranteed to **wreck** his kit each week
    this is a **FREE TRANSFER**
    but he comes with **running expenses**:
10 weeks of washing shirts and shorts
    socks and vests, a pair of trainers
    needs to **scoff** huge amounts
    of chips and **burgers**, beans and apples
    pop and **cola**, crisps and oranges
15 endless packets of chewing gum.
    This offer open until the end of the season
    I'll have him back then
    at least until the cricket starts.
    Any takers?

David Harmer

Word cloud

burgers	pop
cola	scoff
nippy	wreck
nifty	

Understanding

Answer the following questions.

1. What is the literal meaning of this poem?
2. What is the poem's implied meaning?
3. How do you know that this is not a serious poem?
4. In what ways is a love of sport illustrated in the poem?
5. How would you describe your own feelings towards sporting activities in three emotive words?

Glossary

transfer list list of players leaving a club

to dive to cheat by deliberately falling over

penalty box an area marked on the pitch with the goal inside

free transfer to change clubs without paying a fee for the player

running expenses how much something costs to run or look after

any takers? is anyone interested?

Developing your language – using analogy

An analogy is a comparison between two ideas that are alike.

The poem 'My Mum Put Me on the Transfer List' is not meant to be taken literally – the mother does not really want to transfer her son. The poet uses humour and sporting vocabulary to build an analogy of a player being transferred from one club to another. This is used to show the mother's frustration with her son's passion for football.

Answer the following questions.

1. Find three other football-related phrases in the poem.

2. If you were writing a similar poem about a different sport, which sport would you choose? Write down three phrases you would include when creating your analogy.

3. How does making the analogy humorous affect how the reader interprets the implied meaning in the poem?

 Word builder

Answer these questions using words in the Word cloud.

1. How does the use of *nippy* and *nifty* suggest that the boy is good at football? Support your answer with evidence from the poem.

2. Why is *scoff* is more effective than *eat* in this context?

3. How does the more formal meaning of *pop* relate to its informal usage? Use a dictionary to help you.

4. Cola is a word used to give a more general impression than its original meaning. Write down three other words that can be used in this way.

5. *Wreck* is a formal verb but what effect is created by using it informally in the poem?

Key point

Analogies

Using an analogy is a useful way of creating an effect. Comparing a sportsman to a bear makes him sound powerful but slow, whereas comparing him to a cheetah makes him sound fast and agile.

Looking closely

The verb *guaranteed* originated in the late 17th century from either the Spanish word *garante* or the French word *garant* meaning a warrant in legal terms.

A footballer takes a dive in the penalty area

Remember

The vocabulary that you choose to use can affect the way the reader reacts to your writing. Using informal language is a way of making a text sound humorous.

Writing a kenning

You are going to write and present a kenning relating to a sport or a hobby.

A kenning is an old type of poem dating back to Old English and Norse times (790–1066 AD). The idea of kennings is to describe something without using its name. Example of a kenning to describe a javelin:

Javelin

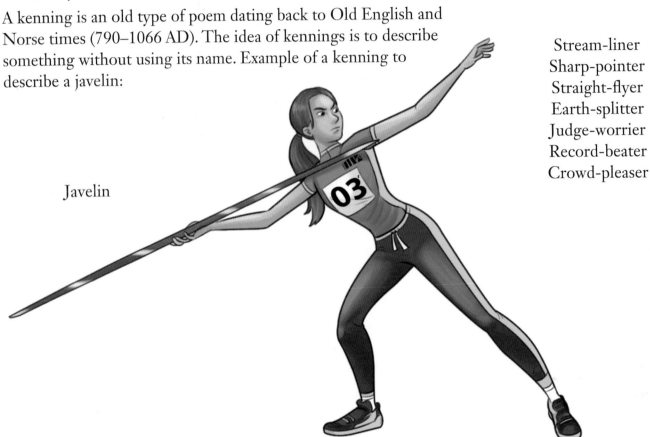

Stream-liner
Sharp-pointer
Straight-flyer
Earth-splitter
Judge-worrier
Record-beater
Crowd-pleaser

Kennings consist of a series of imaginative descriptions that together form an image of the subject. Usually there is one idea per line. Metaphors are often used to build up these descriptions.

Planning your kenning

1. Make a list of suitable subjects for your kenning on the theme of sports or hobbies.

2. Discuss why some subjects work better than others.

3. Experiment with some ideas about subjects you may use for your kenning.

Use the ideas and the planner on the next page to help you. Remember to let your imagination loose!

> **Remember**
>
> A metaphor describes a person or a thing directly as something else.

How to write a kenning

Essentials

The title may contain the subject's name.

There is one central subject.

There is no mention of the subject's name in the body of the text.

Use two-word lines connected by hyphens.

Use metaphors.

Use as many lines as you like.

Extras

Use rhyming couplets.

The description could be a riddle (a puzzling question for the reader to solve). If so, you could use 'What am I?' as the final line.

The shape of the poem could reflect the subject of your description.

Writing frame

1. Write what your chosen subject is

2. List ten qualities of your chosen subject. Each one is going to be one line in your poem. It doesn't matter about the order yet – just start writing ideas.

3. Write only two words to describe each idea.

4. Once you have your ten lines you can put them in order.

5. Write your poem.

Progress check

1. What is the difference between a narrative and non-narrative poem? [2 marks]

2. What is archaic language and why might it be difficult to understand? [2 marks]

3. Virgil's poem about the chariot race is written in what kind of rhyming scheme? How does this work? [2 marks]

4. How many peaks were included in the challenge Hiroto Akiyama completed? Name one of these mountains. [2 marks]

5. Which of these five options match Hiroto's description of how he felt when he first climbed Mount Fuji?

   frightened   exhilarated   like a superhero
       underwhelmed   exhausted   [2 marks]

6. Name the two different types of homonym. Give an example of each. [4 marks]

7. There are two layers of meaning in 'My Mum Put Me on the Transfer List'. What are they? [4 marks]

8. Which two words are most often used to connect the ideas in a simile? Give an example using each one. [4 marks]

9. One of the following phrases is a metaphor and the other is a simile.

   Proud as a peacock strutting his stuff

   The proud peacock strutting his stuff

   Using these examples, explain the difference between a simile and a metaphor. [4 marks]

10. Describe and explain two advantages of using analogy when writing a poem. [4 marks]

3

Reflecting on your learning – writing a successful kenning

Which of the following describes your experience in writing the kenning?

No help needed:
I found it easy

I needed a little help
with my ideas

I made a start

It was hard but I did
it on my own

I needed lots of help
to write it

Action plan

Choose a part of this unit where your understanding was weaker.

Think of improving this area as a race.

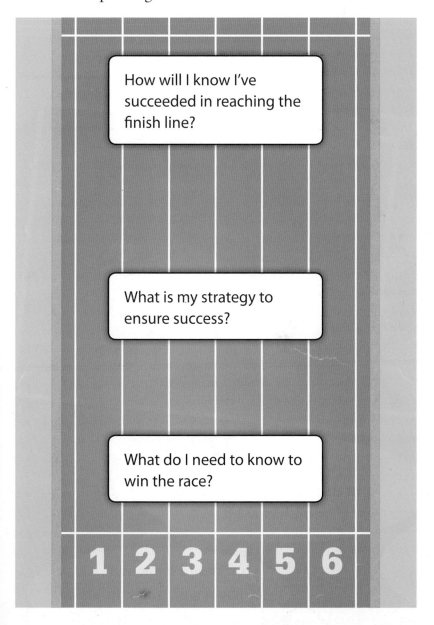

How will I know I've
succeeded in reaching the
finish line?

What is my strategy to
ensure success?

What do I need to know to
win the race?

1 2 3 4 5 6

4 Food for thought

In this unit you will:

Explore
- healthy eating options
- an alternative way to exercise

Create
- a persuasive blog post
- your own examples of imperatives, antithesis and the 'rule of three'

Engage
- with a healthy dish from Lebanon's culture
- with the difficulties facing a village in Africa

Collaborate
- by playing a speaking and listening game to practise the 'rule of three'
- to plan a persuasive blog post for a health or fitness campaign

Reflect
- on the importance of eating a healthy diet
- on how to write non-fiction successfully

You are what you eat

It is important to eat a healthy diet to live a long and happy life.

I don't pay attention to all that healthy eating nonsense – I eat what I want to.

Food hygiene is an important factor in staying healthy.

Thinking time

The World Health Organisation states there are five keys to a healthy diet. These include eating a variety of food, moderate amounts of fats, and less salt and sugars.

1. Why is eating a healthy diet important?
2. What part does regular exercise play in staying healthy?
3. Name five healthy foods and five unhealthy foods.

Speaking and listening

Discuss which of the quotations you agree with. Explain why.

Facts and opinions

Facts

Facts are statements that can be proven with evidence. **Non-fiction** is based on real events, places, and people.

Opinions

Opinions are views or beliefs. They are not necessarily based on facts. Most writers use opinions in their writing to persuade their readers.

Using facts and opinions

Answer the following questions.

1. List five facts and five opinions about the room you are in.
2. Draw a table with two columns – 'Facts' and 'Opinions'. Read the extract and complete your table.

> My name is Kameel. I think eating meat is unhealthy. I eat five portions of vegetables every day and that makes me feel good. I eat fish as I don't think being a vegan is good for you. My friend Samah thinks I'm missing out. She loves chicken.

3. Identify the facts and opinions in the quotations on the opposite page.

OPINION

A recipe for imperatives

A recipe is a non-fiction text. The ingredients and the method are facts. In this recipe the writer's opinions are given in describing the salad as *healthy* and the vegetables as *unique*.

Healthy Lebanese fattoush salad

This healthy, crispy, and crunchy Lebanese salad includes pita bread and unique vegetables such as radish and spring onions. Remember to **toss** the bread in the dressing only a few minutes before you **serve** it or else the bread will soak up the liquid and become soggy.
Preparation time: 10 minutes
Cooking time: 1 to 2 minutes
Makes 4 servings

Ingredients

- 1 pita bread
- 1 cup cucumber, cubed
- 1 cup tomato, cubed
- $\frac{1}{2}$ cup capsicum, cubed
- 1 cup iceberg lettuce, torn into pieces
- $\frac{1}{4}$ cup finely chopped parsley
- $\frac{1}{4}$ cup chopped mint leaves (phudina)
- $\frac{1}{4}$ cup thinly sliced radish (mooli)
- $\frac{1}{4}$ cup thinly sliced spring onion whites
- $\frac{1}{4}$ cup finely chopped spring onion greens

To be mixed into a dressing:

- 2 tbsp olive oil
- 2 tbsp lemon juice
- Salt to taste
- 1 tsp freshly ground black pepper (kali mirch)
- 1 tbsp chopped garlic (lehsun)

Method

- **Toast** the pita bread on a tava (griddle), till it turns golden brown and crispy.
- **Break** it into small pieces and keep aside.
- **Combine** all the ingredients except the bread and toss well.
- **Refrigerate** to chill.
- Just before serving, combine the bread and dressing and toss well.
- Serve immediately.

Based on a recipe by Tarla Dalal: www.tarladalal.com

Understanding

Answer the following questions.

1. What is the purpose of a recipe?

2. What is the effect of using *crispy*, *crunchy*, and *unique* in the first sentence?

3. Suggest why this recipe is easy to follow for someone not used to preparing food.

Key concept

Imperatives

Imperatives are commands. They are often used in writing to instruct or persuade the reader. **Example:**

> You could add garlic after the onions turn brown.

> *becomes*

> Add garlic after onions turn brown.

Developing your language – using imperatives

Rewrite the following sentences using imperatives.

1. Could you stop talking please?

2. You're not really allowed to walk on the grass.

3. I wouldn't swim there – I think there's a shark nearby!

Word builder

Answer these questions.

1. The words in the Word cloud are used as imperatives in the recipe.

   a Why are most of the imperatives found in the 'Method' section?

   b Why is the imperative placed at the beginning of the phrase?

   c Write an instruction using *soak* as an imperative.

2. Write three imperatives that the people in the pictures might use.

Word cloud

break	serve
combine	toast
refrigerate	toss

Glossary

capsicum a kind of pepper (used here as a vegetable not a spice)

tbsp tablespoon

tsp teaspoon

Teachers

Police officers

Fitness instructors

The 'rule of three'

In these phrases, the ideas are grouped into threes.

- He's a lean, mean, eating machine!
- Eat less fatty food, drink more water and exercise frequently.
- Chill out! Stay calm! Relax!

Key concept

The rule of three

The **rule of three** is a technique used to stress the importance of certain points – we see a pattern and this helps us to remember the point being made. This is also called the 'use of a triad'.

Oh, it's an elephant.

Oh, there's two elephants.

Three elephants!

Answer the following questions.

1. Complete these examples of the rule of three.

    a The boy was lazy, disinterested, and _____.

    b Vote for me for team captain because I am intelligent, caring, and _____.

    c I love field hockey because it is exciting, thrilling, and _____.

    d My face is washed, my hair is combed, and _____.

2. Write sentences using the rule of three. Use the following beginnings:

    a I am...

    b My best friend is...

    c My favourite film star is...

3. What tips would you give a younger student about using the rule of three successfully?

Tricolons

Tricolons are a series of three words, phrases, or clauses of the same length, used in the rule of three.

A famous tricolon was created by the Roman general and emperor, Julius Caesar. Describing an important victory he wrote: *Veni, vidi, vici* (Latin for 'I came, I saw, I conquered').

This example uses alliteration.

'*Slip* (on a shirt), *slop* (on some sun cream), *slap* (on a hat)'

Using tricolons

Answer these questions.

1. For each of the tricolons below, suggest what it means and the context in which it is used. Use the Internet to help you.

   a Lights, camera, action.

   b Stop, look, listen.

   c Work, rest, play.

   d Past, present, future.

2. Create catchphrases using tricolons for each of the following advertising campaigns:

   a A brand new healthy snack

   b A new piece of healthy exercise equipment

   c A new health treatment

The rule of three game

You can have a lot of fun with triads. Here are the rules to a simple game you can play in a pair or a group.

- Player A nominates a subject. (Player C must not be able to hear what Player A says.)

- Player B has to describe the subject within 15 seconds using the rule of three.

- Player C has 15 seconds to think of an answer.

Example:

Player A: Tigers

Player B: Feline, ferocious, and frightening. *Player B gets three points for accurately using three descriptions of tigers.*

Player C is awarded five points if they can correctly identify the subject.

After an agreed amount of time the winner is the player with the most points.

 **Looking closely**

Triad is originally from the Greek word *trias,* meaning group of three, and *tricolon* comes from two Greek words meaning three and unit.

Persuasive writing

Read the following article about the benefits of yoga.

Yoga: Relax and be healthy

1 Is life getting you stressed? Don't let it! Try yoga. Feel good again!

Is this you?

Your husband is working late again; your baby won't stop crying and your mother-in-law is visiting tomorrow. You feel anxious all
5 the time. If this sounds like you, give yoga a try.

What is yoga?

Yoga has been around for thousands of years. It is a **holistic** approach that consists of easily attainable **calisthenics** to improve **core strength** whilst controlling your **respiratory** function and
10 relaxing your **cognitive** state. Yoga can help reduce stress, counter **hypertension** and improve **cardio-vascular** exertion.

Is it for me?

Almost anyone can practise yoga. Not only can it reduce stress and anxiety but it can also make you feel less tired and much
15 calmer, meaning you can confidently face all that life throws at you. Start by trying Hatha as it is one of the most popular forms of yoga and is ideal for melting all that stress. It's also slower-paced than other forms and so is ideal for beginners.

Where do I do it?

20 You can practise yoga anywhere you can lay your mat and relax but first you should join a local class to learn the basic postures – and how to practise them safely.

What will I be doing?

You will begin by learning a number of simple postures that increase
25 your **flexibility** by building your body strength. You will learn to control your breathing, relax your mind, and find inner peace.

So what are you waiting for? Why don't you get out there and try it!

Understanding

Using the article, answer these questions.

1. Where is an ideal place to go to start practising yoga?
2. How does the writer persuade readers that yoga improves health?
3. Give two benefits of learning to control your breathing using yoga?

Word cloud

calisthenics
cardio-vascular
cognitive
core strength
flexibility
holistic
hypertension
respiratory

Developing your language – being persuasive

Some texts leave you in no doubt what the writer wants you to think. Read this extract by a critic of yoga.

http://www.health_chat.com/messages

Make no mistake about it, yoga is bad for you. All that stretching only leads to pulled muscles, torn ligaments, and backache. Yes, it's bad for you! Try a brisk healthy walk or a slow gentle jog if you want to reduce stress, increase your fitness, and feel good. Yoga's just another trend that makes promises it can't deliver. And don't be fooled by all those 'it is very old so must be good for you' comments. Modern yoga isn't old and it isn't good for you. Believe me, I've tried it!

This is a biased negative account and makes no attempt to offer a balanced argument. The writer of this article wants you to dislike yoga as much as she does.

Using the two extracts about yoga, write a balanced article about what yoga is, and what some people think about it.

 ## Word builder

Jargon is language used by some people, for example in one profession, that may be difficult for others to understand. Choosing your vocabulary carefully is important. In persuasive writing, using jargon can be very effective in convincing a reader that you are an expert on the subject you are writing about.

The terms in the Word cloud are examples of jargon often used to describe the effects of exercise on the body.

Use the terms in the Word cloud to answer these questions.

1. Are any of the terms not in the dictionary? If so, why do you think this is?

2. *Cardio-vascular* refers to heart and lung functions and *hypertension* is a technical term for high blood pressure. Suggest why the writer did not use simpler terms.

3. Seven of the eight words appear in the same paragraph near the beginning of the article. What effect does this create?

Opposites attract

Antithesis (pronounced *an-tith-iss-iss*) occurs when two contrasting or opposite ideas are used together. **Example:**

> The night was cold but the day was warm.
>
> Polar bears may look cute and cuddly but they are dangerous and deadly predators.

When using antitheses, writers contrast a powerful idea against a weaker one. In the examples above, the second idea has more influence on the reader.

Changing the order shifts the emphasis. **Example:**

> The day was warm but the night was cold.
>
> Polar bears are dangerous and deadly but they look cute and cuddly.

Looking closely

Antithesis is Greek in origin and comes from two words joined together. *Anti* means against and *thesis* means placing.

Answer the following questions.

1. Write four sentences using antithesis to describe the following:

   a hot/cold

   b fast/slow

2. Change the emphasis in your sentences from **1** by reordering the clauses.

Who are you calling cute and cuddly?

Using antithesis in your work and play

Read the opening section of 'Is this you?' in the article about yoga (page 56).

In this antithesis the problems are written first, using two sentences and the rule of three. The solution follows, to persuade the reader that doing yoga would solve these problems.

Read these extracts and answer the questions.

A All that stretching only leads to pulled muscles, torn ligaments and backache. Yes, it's bad for you! Try a brisk healthy walk or a slow gentle jog if you want to reduce stress, increase your fitness, and feel good.

B The desert is vast, empty, hot, arid and not at all welcoming. Water is difficult to find. Hardly any life can survive in this desolate landscape. Kilometres of nothing but burning sand threaten you in every direction.

1. Explain the effect of the use of antithesis in Extract A.

2. Write a paragraph that is the antithesis to the description of the desert in Extract B.

Two antithesis games

Opposites attract

Before starting, players agree a time. Player 1 says a word. Within five seconds, Player 2 has to say a word meaning the opposite. Players take it in turns to say a starting word. Every correct response earns 1 point. Whoever has most points when the time is up wins.

The five-minute challenge

Players agree on a subject for a five-minute conversation. Player 1 makes a comment. Player 2 gives a contrasting idea. Then Player 1 speaks again, and so on. The player unable to sustain the conversation loses. **Example:**

Player 1: "I love the creamy taste of chocolate."

Player 2: "Yes, but it's so sickly."

Player 1: "It isn't if you eat only a little at a time."

Player 2: "But it's full of sugar and even a little is bad for you."

The Moroccan Sahara Desert

'Matumaini' – a radio charity appeal

A dried-up river bed in Kenya

Listen to 'Matumaini' – a radio advertisement produced by the charity Hopeful Springs. You will hear the male narrator's voice first then the voice of the female charity worker.

Understanding

Listen carefully to the recording and answer these questions.

1. What and where is Matumaini?
2. Why is Matumaini a difficult place in which to help people?
3. What is the effect of hearing two voices in the appeal?
4. Would this advertisement make you want to help the people of Matumaini by making a donation?

Glossary

drought a long period when there is little or no rain

fetid unpleasant smelling

irrigate to supply with water (usually land or crops)

lifeblood the source of life

malevolence evil

malnutrition illness caused by lack of food

predatory preying on others

Key concept

Rhetorical questions

Rhetorical questions are questions asked in order to make a point rather than to prompt an answer. They are very useful when writing to persuade. **Example:**

"This is a small price to pay for life, hope and good health, wouldn't you agree?"

Remember

Sometimes adverbs can be used with adjectives to add emphasis to a description. **Example:** *pitifully inadequate.*

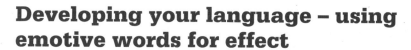

Developing your language – using emotive words for effect

'Matumaini' is a charity appeal. It uses language designed to create an emotional response in the audience.

I can't breathe!

In his first sentence the narrator describes the months as *stifling*. The scriptwriter could have used *hot* but that would have only told part of the story. *Stifling* suggests the weather is not just hot but suffocating. It is more emotive and effective because it paints an image of the villagers straining to breathe because of the heat.

Write an appeal for something you are passionate about. Remember to use emotive words for effect.

 Word builder

Answer these questions.

1. Identify the word in the Word cloud with a positive connotation. Suggest its meaning.

2. Choose five words from the Word cloud and find them in a thesaurus. Write down a list of alternative words for each one.

3. For each of your five words, decide on the alternative that is most effective. Explain your answer.

4. Rewrite this extract using alternative emotive words for those in bold.

1 The **burning** sun made my nerve-endings tingle. I made a **desperate** attempt to avoid the **stifling** heat. My inadequate hat didn't stop my head feeling as if it was on fire and the **meagre**
5 shade I found didn't ease my discomfort. After three days in the **unremitting** desert without food or water I felt **emaciated** and badly in need of a **precious** drink. Finally, I came across a pool. The water was **stagnant** but at least I would survive. 10

Writing a persuasive blog post

A blog post is a piece of writing that appears on a website. A collection of these posts forms a blog.

Plan and write a blog post designed to persuade your readers to agree to your opinions.

Use the guidance provided to help you.

Persuasive features

- facts and opinions
- imperatives
- antithesis
- the rule of three
- emotive language

Your blog post should support one of the following campaigns:

- healthy eating in your school or college
- a charity raising funds to run community fitness classes
- a sponsored sports event to raise funds for your school or college
- bringing doctors into schools on a regular basis to teach healthy living.

Planning your blog post

Think of as many reasons as you can why a reader should consider your chosen campaign. Consider what evidence could be used to support each reason and different ways to make your appeal convincing.

The stronger your argument, the more persuasive it will be.

Use the framework opposite to help you to plan your response.

Writing framework for the blog post

Introduction

- Explain what campaign you are supporting and give a general reason why the reader should support it too.
- Use a rhetorical question.
- Write in the first person.
- Speak directly to the reader.
- Make your blog post dramatic.

Argument 1

- Explain what the problem is, why it needs fixing, and how you propose to do this.
- Make one clear point and explain in detail using supporting evidence.
- Use emotive language and as many other persuasive features as you can to make the reader feel sympathetic.

Argument 2

- Introduce your second point.
- Repeat the process of explaining the issue in detail, why it needs fixing, and how you propose to do this.
- Use supporting evidence.
- Use a variety of persuasive features. Remember that repeating an idea in different words, or repeating a particularly emotive phrase, can be very effective in persuading the reader.

The appeal

- Write directly to the reader.
- Use rhetorical questions to influence the reader's viewpoint.
- Make your appeal sensible and polite.
- Be practical in what you ask of the reader.

Checklist

1 Have you used supporting evidence to give authority to your views?

Have you scanned your blog post for evidence of persuasive features, as on page 62? Have you used them all?

Would you respond positively to this appeal if you were the reader?

Progress check

1. According to the World Health Organisation, what are two of the keys to a healthy diet? [2 marks]

2. What two features of its structure make a recipe easy to follow? [2 marks]

3. Give two reasons why a dish such as fattoush salad may be considered healthy. [2 marks]

4. How does antithesis work? Give an example. [2 marks]

5. *Matumaini* is a Swahili word. What does it mean in English? Why is the name appropriate for the charity appeal? [2 marks]

6. What is the purpose of an imperative? Where is it usually placed in a phrase or sentence? Give two examples of sentences containing imperatives. [4 marks]

7. What is a fact? Why is it different from an opinion? Give an example of each. [4 marks]

8. Explain the rule of three. Write down two examples. [4 marks]

9. What is emotive language and what response does it create in its audience? Why is it used in the charity appeal? [4 marks]

10. When planning a piece of persuasive writing, what four features should you plan to include? [4 marks]

Reflecting on your learning – non-fiction writing

Copy and complete the following table.

When writing a blog post I can:	I fully understand	I think I do	I'm not really sure
use a writing framework to plan my blog			
clearly explain what campaign I am supporting			
speak directly to my reader			
use evidence to support my points			
use emotive language to persuade my reader			
ensure my language is polite and appropriate for my audience			

My action plan

Thinking about where I've placed myself on the table:

1. Is this an accurate view of my progress?
2. Which of the writing skills did I struggle with?
3. What can I do better to improve my position on the table?
4. How am I going to do this?

Explore
- real and imagined journeys
- a 19th-century railway journey in India

Create
- a piece of descriptive writing
- a news report about a strange event on your way to school

Engage
- with words in English borrowed from another culture
- with children talking about their views on holidays

Collaborate
- on the pleasures and the hardships of travel
- in experimenting with vowel sounds

In this chapter you will:

Reflect
- on different accounts of journeys
- on the dangers of cycling

I like visiting different places, but I must admit I don't like aeroplanes and airports.

My parents travelled a lot to do with their work and I had to go with them. I think being dragged from place to place has affected me and I don't enjoy travelling now I'm older.

You meet people when you travel, and you have your mind opened to new ideas.

Thinking time

Today, people have opportunities to travel that their ancestors could never have dreamed of. Look at the quotations and photographs opposite. Answer these questions.

1. Do you agree with any of them? Why?

2. What do you think of journeys to distant places?

3. Is getting to a place often more interesting than being there? Explain your answer.

Remember

A blog is a regularly updated website that records experiences and opinions.

Word cloud

bulging	pouring
flickered	torrential
drenched	

A travel blog post

http://www.inntravel.co.uk

1 As our two boys slept on the back seat of the hire car, exhausted from their early morning plane-spotting at the airport, lightning **flickered** across **bulging** grey-black clouds,
5 then **torrential** rain began to cascade down the windscreen. It was still **pouring** by the time we pulled up at the **Catalan** farmhouse. We sat immobile in our seats, our reluctance to get **drenched** outweighing our eagerness to
10 explore our holiday home. Then a figure, clad from head to foot in shiny yellow **oilskins** and holding two **golfing umbrellas**, dashed across the yard and introduced himself to us as David, one of the owners. Offering us the umbrellas, he grabbed one of our cases from the boot 15 and ran with us to our first-floor apartment, a stylish blend of exposed stone walls, contemporary kitchen and attractive furniture.

From A is for animals, B is for beaches, C is for castles by Beth Hancock, Inntravel.

Word builder

Use the words in the Word cloud to complete the following sentences.

1. After suffering a flash storm we were _____.

2. The very dark rain clouds indicated that we might be in for showers which could be _____.

3. As the storm passed over the farmhouse, the lights in the house _____.

4. The clouds we drove through seemed to be _____ just before the rain fell.

Glossary

Catalan from Catalonia, a region in north-east Spain

oilskins outdoor waterproofed clothes

golfing umbrellas large umbrellas, used by golfers

Around the world in 80 days

Read this account of Phileas Fogg in his attempt to travel around the world in 80 days, before the days of aeroplanes.

Fogg meets Kiouni

1   He was actually crossing India in a railway train! It threw out its smoke upon cotton, coffee, nutmeg, clove, and pepper plantations, while the steam curled in spirals around groups of palm-trees, in the midst of which were seen **picturesque** bungalows,

5   viharis (sort of abandoned monasteries), and marvellous temples enriched by the exhaustless **ornamentation** of Indian architecture. Then they came upon jungles **inhabited** by snakes and tigers, which fled at the noise of the train; succeeded by forests penetrated by the railway,

10   and still **haunted** by elephants which, with pensive eyes, gazed at the train as it passed. …

The train stopped, at eight o'clock, in the midst of a glade some fifteen miles beyond Rothal, where there were several bungalows, and workmen's cabins. The **conductor**, passing

15   along the carriages, shouted, "Passengers will get out here!"

… The railway came to a **termination** at this point. The papers were too fast in their announcement of the completion of the line. Travellers began to engage such vehicles as the village four-wheeled wagons drawn by zebus, carriages that

20   looked like perambulating pagodas, and an elephant!

The elephant, which its owner had reared, not for a beast of burden, but for warlike purposes, was half domesticated and still preserved his natural gentleness. Kiouni could doubtless travel rapidly for a long time, and Mr. Fogg resolved to hire him. …

25   At two thousand pounds the owner yielded.

"What a price, good heavens!" cried Passepartout, "for an elephant".

A young guide offered his services, which Mr. Fogg accepted, promising a generous **reward**. The guide **perched** himself on the elephant's neck, and at nine o'clock they set out from the

30   village, the animal marching off through the dense forest of palms by the shortest cut.

From *Around the World in 80 Days* by Jules Verne

Word cloud

conductor
haunted
inhabited
ornamentation
perched
picturesque
reward
termination

Understanding

Answer the following questions.

1. Which two types of natural environment does the train travel through?

2. Why did passengers leave the train 15 miles beyond Rothal?

3. How do some passengers continue the rest of their journey?

Remember

A simile is a way of comparing a person or thing to something else, usually using words such as *like* and *as*.

Context clues

Look again at this sentence:

Travellers began to engage such vehicles as the village four-wheeled wagons drawn by zebus, carriages that looked like perambulating pagodas…

From the context of the text, we know that *wagons* must be a form of transport from *such vehicles*.

We cannot guess what pagodas are, however. A carriage looks like a pagoda, but unless we know what a pagoda is, the simile is not helpful.

We can guess that the wagons are probably pulled by animals from *drawn by zebus*.

Suggest definitions for the made-up words (in italics) using context clues.

1. As the train stopped suddenly, a large crunching noise was heard coming from its *collybonter*.

2. I overheard a passenger complaining about the food to the *popplecrake*.

3. Although we'd waited only an hour to catch our elephant, it felt like a *bod*.

4. Write two sentences using made-up words about travel or transport. Give definitions for your new words.

🧩 Word builder

Answer the following questions using context clues.

1. Describe the architecture in the extract.

2. Write down a word to replace *termination*, given the sentences before and after it.

Vowels and double consonants

- The five vowels in English are: *a*, *e*, *i*, *o*, and *u*
- All other letters in the alphabet are consonants.

Note that *y* can also play the role of a vowel in words such as *try* and *fly*.

Pronouncing vowels

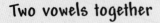

Short vowels	Long vowels
These are snappy.	These are drawn out.
(*ticket, rig, hop*)	(*fare, dive, stroll*)

Two vowels together

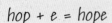

These make one sound.

(*train, boat, leap*)

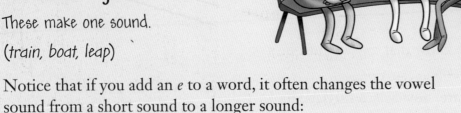

Notice that if you add an *e* to a word, it often changes the vowel sound from a short sound to a longer sound:

hop + e = hope   bath + e = bathe   din + e = dine

If a word has a short vowel and more than one syllable, the vowel is often followed by a double consonant:

cattle   apple   bigger

Carry out the following activities. Do not use the examples above.

1. Write a set of three words with a similar theme but different vowel sounds: one with a short vowel sound, one with a long sound, and one with two vowels together that make one sound.

2. Think of a word that ends in a consonant. Add an *e*. If your new word makes sense, write it down.

3. Adding an *e* to a word often changes the vowel sound from a short sound to a longer sound. List two exceptions to this rule.

4. Think of three words that start with a short vowel sound and have more than one syllable. How many of them use double consonants?

Vowel and consonant challenge

In this extract from *Around the World in 80 Days*, Phileas Fogg, Passepartout, and a lady called Aouda (rescued by the men along the way) are crossing the Pacific Ocean. They avoid disaster and stay afloat despite the storms.

All at Sea

… The night was really terrible; it would be a miracle if the craft **did not founder**. Twice it could have been all over with her if the crew had not been constantly on the watch. Aouda was exhausted, but did not utter a complaint. More than once Mr. Fogg rushed to protect her from the violence of the waves.

… Day appeared. **The tempest still raged** with **undiminished fury**; but the wind now returned to the south-east. It was a favourable change, and the Tankadere again bounded forward on this **mountainous sea**, though the waves crossed each other, and imparted shocks and counter-shocks which would have crushed a craft less solidly built.

From *Around the World in 80 Days* by Jules Verne

Read the rules, then decide on a number for your answer to each question.

Rules

1. You are not allowed to include proper nouns!

2. You cannot use the same word twice!

1. How many words can you find in the extract with long vowel sounds?

2. How many words of no more than two syllables have short vowel sounds using *u*?

3. How many words have double consonants?

4. Add up the numbers from **1–3**. This is your score. Compare your score with others.

Glossary

did not founder did not fill with water then sink

the tempest still raged the violent storm continued

undiminished fury anger that was not decreasing

mountainous sea sea with huge waves

 The excitement of travel

Listen to this discussion between Hanna and Mia about their views on travelling.

Understanding

Answer the following questions.

1. How do Hanna and Mia feel about the time running up to a journey?

2. Do they feel any differently about airports and flying?

3. How do they feel about travel to far-off places?

4. Where is it that Hanna and Mia believe you should open up your mind most?

5. What do they think are the pros and cons of travelling when they are older?

 The journey to school

We often think of journeys as being an adventure, even though many of them in our everyday lives are very routine and repetitive. Look at the pictures of children going to school.

Role-play these journeys to school.

One of you is the interviewer, asking about these journeys. Talk about these journeys to school and compare with your own journeys.

Developing your language – describing your favourite walk

Read this student's account of his favourite walk.

Answer the questions that follow.

> 1   My favourite walk is a circular walk around a small town. I start from the
>   lower end of the oldest street in the town, with cobbled streets, dating back
>   to the 18th century. On something of a climb, I head up Bank Street, where
>   there are dilapidated buildings being restored. Still heading up towards
> 5   the top of town, I go through the town gate. Now on the flat, I turn right
>   and walk along Welsh Street until I come to the footpath that will take me
>   alongside the castle, which is 1000 years old. It's always shady and cold here,
>   never a place to stop for long.
>   The path then sweeps down to a car park and the tourist office, where I
> 10 turn left onto Bridge Street. The 19th-century bridge is in front of me now.
>   I turn right and walk along the riverside for a short way... .

1. Write a list of adjectives used in this extract.

2. Explain the importance of using adjectives when describing your favourite walk.

3. Write an account of your favourite walk. Use the same style as in the extract, so that readers can imagine following your footsteps.

Punctuation – stop, start, pause…

Think about choosing the best punctuation mark at each point in your writing like driving a train – you need to know when to start, when to stop, and when to slow down.

Full stops

Concentrate first on the full stop (which stops a series of words). **Example:**

Phileas Fogg went around the world. He had many adventures.

Commas

Commas are used to pause or slow down a series of words. Rules for using commas are more flexible than those for full stops.

- Commas separate items in a list: Phileas Fogg travelled through Europe, Asia, and America.

- Commas appear between parts of sentences (phrases or clauses): Although Passepartout was his servant, Phileas Fogg treated him like a friend.

- Commas sometimes work as pairs (like brackets): Jules Verne, who was French, is one of the most translated writers.

- Commas appear after a connecting word, at the start of a sentence: However, Jules Verne did not travel to many of the countries he wrote about.

Remember

Punctuation is the use of special marks to make a piece of writing easier to read or to understand.

Add the correct punctuation to the following sentences.

1. The train came 20 minutes early so I caught it and got to Delhi in good time to meet my friends

2. The train came 20 minutes late as a result I missed meeting up with my friends

The stop-start punctuation challenge

Play the following game in groups.

1. Write a sentence of about 30 words related to a journey but without any punctuation.

2. Pass your sentence to another person.

3. Add commas and full stops where they are needed in the sentence you are given.

4. Pass the sentence back to the original writer, who reads the new version aloud.

   For this to work, only pause where there is punctuation.

Key concept

Questions and exclamations

Question marks (?) and exclamation marks (!) also stop readers in their tracks.

1. A **direct question** asks for information and requires an answer. A question ends with a question mark. **Example:**

   "Is the train from Delhi on time?"

2. An **indirect** or **reported question** uses a full stop. **Example:**

   The conductor asked them what their names were.

3. An **exclamation** is normally a short sentence that expresses a strong or sudden feeling and ends in an exclamation mark. **Example:** "

   I can't believe the train from Delhi is that late!"

4. A **command** tells someone to do something. You can use an exclamation mark to make the command more forceful. **Example:**

   Do not cross the railway tracks!

Using question marks and exclamation marks

Answer the following questions.

1. Copy the newspaper report below, adding question marks and exclamation marks where required.

   I wondered how many days it had taken the train to arrive at its destination The carriages were stunning I had been waiting for several hours in the heat with the other reporters to report on this memorable event Was that the King I could see in the leading carriage As I moved forward to get a better look I saw the sign Keep clear of the Royal Carriage

"Where should I go?"

"Let's get into position!"

2. For each of the following scenarios write a short paragraph including a direct and an indirect question, an exclamation and a command.

   a Travelling across the desert on a camel

   b Travelling on the very first commercial aeroplane from New York to London

   c Taking part in a motor car race

It's all about the bike

In this extract, Robert Penn writes of a high-speed 'blow-out' he experienced when cycling.

1   A high-speed 'blow-out', when the tyre bursts spectacularly with the sound of a gunshot, is one of the things road cyclists fear the most. If you are **dropping like a stone** down a mountain road, you can be thrown from the bike.

5   The one dramatic blow-out I had that still gives me flashbacks was in the Fergana Mountains in Kyrgystan. I was coming down from a pass on a gravel road, on a loaded touring bike. When the **hairpins** finished, and the road opened out before me, I let the brakes go. **At full tilt**, the front tyre – a cheap locally made tyre

10 I'd bought in the market in Kashgar – blew. The bike slid briefly, then the handlebar **jack-knifed** and I was off. Somehow, the bike was **propelled** into the air. As it came down on top of me, the teeth of the chainrings **scalped** the side of my head.

A few hours later, I reached a farm on the road – the first

15 settlement I'd seen all day. Blood **congealed** with dust covered the side of my face. My shirt was **shredded**. I leant my bike against the gate and walked up the path. Children and women scattered, shrieking. The farmer, a **barrel-chested** Kyrgyz man with taut, mongoloid features, appeared from the shadows with

20 a pistol at the end of his stiff arm. I tried a few words of Russian. No reply. Then his eyes **flickered** past me to the gate, and my bicycle. The pistol arm fell limp. The leathery brown skin on his face re-set to a broad grin. Ten minutes later, I was eating kebabs and yoghurt as his wife **sponged** blood from my head. I had the

25 bicycle to thank for my salvation: it was the last time I would ever **grace** it with a cheap tyre.

From *It's All About the Bike: The Pursuit of Happiness of Two Wheels* by Robert Penn

Word cloud

congealed	scalped
flickered	shredded
jack-knifed	sponged
propelled	

Glossary

at full tilt full speed

barrel-chested having a large, rounded chest

drop like a stone to move quickly downwards

grace it with to give it

hairpins sharp turns in a road

Understanding

Answer the following questions.

1. What were the risks and dangers faced by Penn in this passage?

2. How do you think he would respond to each of those risks and dangers?

3. Why was the farmer nervous when Penn arrived at the gate of his farm?

4. Explain the reaction of the children and women.

5. What are your thoughts and feelings about the farmer and his family?

Key concept

Active and passive verbs

Verbs can be divided into two groups:

● **Active** verbs are used when the subject of the sentence does the action. **Example:**

   When the tyre bursts...

● **Passive** verbs are used when the action is done to the subject. **Example**:

   You can be thrown from a bike...

Active verb

Developing your language – active and passive verbs

Answer the questions that follow.

1. Identify the verbs in the sentence below as active or passive.

   Robert's wounds were tended to by the farmer's wife, while the farmer repaired his puncture.

2. Copy and complete these sentences by adding verbs. The subject is underlined.

   a The <u>farmer</u> was _____ when he saw the accident, and the <u>crop</u> had been _____ by his reaction.

   b The <u>truck driver</u> was being _____ by the farmer's wife as he was in shock after seeing <u>Robert</u> _____ towards him.

   c The <u>journey</u> would have been _____ by 5 p.m. but after the crash Robert had to _____ the journey for the day.

 **Word builder**

Action verbs show something happening.

Use the Word cloud to complete the paragraph on the right.

Passive verb

I left Almaty in the morning and noticed my tyres had become covered with a thick liquid which had __1__ overnight. However, I continued my journey as I had to get the vegetables to Ust Kamenogorsk by nightfall. About two hours later I saw a cyclist. He had fallen off his bicycle. As my eyes __2__ quickly, I could see his tyre was __3__. I braked too hard and __4__ my truck. It stopped just in front of the cyclist but the force of braking __5__ me into the windscreen.

Writing a descriptive account

Creating a sense of place

Creating 'a sense of place' in writing is like painting a picture in words. It is very limiting to use only adjectives and adverbs in descriptive writing, as they can be overused. **Example:**

A On her way to Freddo's coffee shop, the frail, old lady with her crooked, wooden stick walked slowly and painfully down the long tree-lined avenue with the golden sun beating heartlessly down on her from an azure-blue sky.

However, nouns and verbs can also add to descriptive language. **Example:**

B Freddo's tiny coffee shop was located on one of Amsterdam's canals, or, as the Dutch say, grachts. Despite its size, it was always full of people. It was on the corner of a busy street and, no matter where you sat, you had a great view of city life right outside the window. Once you got to know it, you were more than tempted to come back...

Try to see, in your mind's eye, what you are describing when you write about real places and people.

Look at the two extracts and answer these questions.

1. Remove as many descriptive words as you can from Extract A without changing the meaning.

2. Identify the nouns used in Extract B to describe Freddo's coffee shop.

3. Write Extract A again, but in the style of Extract B.

Imagining the scene

A key to creating a good sense of place is to imagine yourself at the scene you are describing. You can improve your descriptive writing using the following tips:

- People feature in many scenes. In a busy scene, the people may appear as a crowd, without any sense of individuality. You should therefore avoid generalising people in a scene.

- Short sections of dialogue can also work, for example, Freddo shouting "Tall latte!" or a quick humorous exchange.

- Think about the weather. Its description is often used to set the scene.

- Include sensory language **(details of what can be seen, heard, felt, tasted and smelled)** to make your writing more realistic and descriptive.

Answer the following questions.

1. Write two descriptive sentences about individual people in Freddo's coffee shop.

2. Write a simple, single exchange between two people in the coffee shop.

3. Write two sentences describing the weather and how it has an impact on events in the coffee shop.

4. Think of something in the shop that involves movement. Describe it as carefully as you can.

Your descriptive account

Your descriptive account should be around 200 words. Use the following suggestions to help you.

1. Choose a location in which to set your scene. Make sure that there are people present and that there is some activity. Give yourself enough to describe!

2. Focus on all of your senses so that your writing has depth and added interest.

3. Include movement, such as yourself walking through the scene.

4. Use as many descriptive writing devices as you can.

Progress check

1. Where are you most likely to see blogs? Give one feature of blog writing. [2 marks]

2. What two modes of transport did Phileas Fogg use in India as part of his journey around the world? [2 marks]

3. What is a context clue, and when would you use it? [2 marks]

4. What are long and short vowels? Give an example of each. [2 marks]

5. What is your favourite part of a holiday? Explain your answer. [2 marks]

6. When would you use an exclamation mark? Give an example of each use. [4 marks]

7. Give four features that you would incorporate when describing a short journey. [4 marks]

8. Give four risks or dangers you might face on a cycling trip in a place you are not familiar with. [4 marks]

9. Name two types of verb you might use when writing a report of an incident. Give an example of each. [4 marks]

10. Write a short descriptive account of a memory or an event. Use four different descriptive features. [4 marks]

Reflecting on your learning – features of descriptive writing

Use the following checklist for your descriptive writing.

1. Have I set the scene effectively in the opening sentences?

↓

2. Have I included interesting people?

↓

3. Have I used a range of simple and complex sentences for effect?

↓

4. Have I used powerful adjectives and adverbs?

↓

5. Have I used exclamation marks to good effect?

↓

6. Have I used sensory language well?

↓

7. Have I used connectives to ensure flow in paragraphs and between paragraphs?

↓

8. Does my ending close the scene well?

Choose three of these points that you think you need to practise more. Or choose two of these and add a new one of your own.

For each point, describe the journey you will go on to improve.

In this unit you will:

Explore
- the experience of acting in a Shakespearian play
- a Punch and Judy show from a hundred years ago

Create
- your own play scene
- a dialogue between Mr Punch and the Bottler

Engage
- with life in the Russian countryside
- with the atmosphere of a street puppet show

Collaborate
- in playing drama games
- in a big plural spelling quiz

Reflect
- on Shakespeare's language
- on how writers present character in drama

All the world's a stage

The problem is that some people live their normal lives as if they were acting in a play.

Drama's about doing and moving, not just reading words on a page.

If it's really dramatic, we can laugh and cry.

Thinking time

Look at the photographs and quotations on the opposite page.

1. What do the photographs make you think about acting? Think about any experiences you have had by being in a play, even a short one.

2. What do the words *drama* and *dramatic* mean?

3. Two of the quotations talk about being in an audience. Which do you prefer? Explain your answer.

4. How can drama be dangerous? Use the quotations to help you.

5. Discuss another quotation about drama that you would like to add.

Speaking and listening

Play the following games involving drama.

1. Who is it?

Get in a group. One person stands at the front with their back to the others. Someone in the group describes another student. The person at the front has to guess who is being described – if it's too difficult then the person at the front can ask questions.

The person described moves to the front of the group. Repeat.

2. Travel agent

Carry out a role-play where one person is a travel agent who arranges people's holidays. The others are customers who have had different experiences on their travels. Some are going to complain, some will say what a great time they have had.

Customers could have experienced:

- long-distance travel
- time travel
- space travel
- a cruise
- an adventure holiday – back packing and exploration.

Don't tell the person playing the travel agent anything in advance!

First night

Read the following extract about a writer's experience of playing a fairy in a Shakespeare play when she was 12 years old.

1   I was a bag of nerves, a 12-year-old waiting for the moment to go on at the beginning of Act 2 of Shakespeare's hilarious play, *A Midsummer Night's Dream* in front of a frighteningly full **auditorium**. It wasn't exactly my sort of English – after all, it
5   was written 400 years ago. You have to know what the words mean and say them loud and clear.

Anyway, I played a fairy. Fairies were much more real in Shakespeare's time, and I had to say this poem to Puck who was the chief servant of Oberon, King of the fairies. The play is all about some women
10   (played by the older girls, of course) getting mixed up by magic with the wrong boyfriends. I was a very minor member of the **cast**.

Back to my story. The curtain went up and I was on. I entered **downstage** with the **spotlight** in my eyes and Puck said "How now spirit, whither wander you?" I had to say this poem without
15   forgetting my lines and needing the **prompter**:

> Over hill, over dale,
> Thorough bush, thorough briar,
> I do wander everywhere.

The **producer** had told me where to move and what expression
20   I should have on my face – I guess I looked as if I was about to faint – fairies don't just stand rooted to the spot, he'd said, because the audience would be bored.

It didn't go badly. The rhymes in the verse helped and I didn't miss anything out. I even got my rhymed couplet right at the end. Then I
25   waited while Puck did his bit and I had another speech about people's belief in hobgoblins – they were so superstitious in those days.

Word cloud

auditorium	producer
cast	prompter
downstage	spotlight

Glossary

bag of nerves completely nervous

rooted to the spot unable to move

rhymed couplet two lines of verse that rhyme

hobgoblin one of many types of spirit believed in in Shakespeare's time

Understanding

Answer the following questions.

1. How did the writer feel before she went on stage?

2. Is the play called *A Midsummer Night's Dream* best described as real-life, boring, or amusing?

3. What did the writer learn about Shakespeare's time?

Word builder

The words in the Word cloud are associated with theatre. **Answer the following questions**.

1. Use the words about theatre below to complete the following paragraph. One has been done for you.

   cue   break a leg   curtain up   audition   wings

   I remember my first time on stage well. I'd been to an ___audition___ to see whether I was any good. Before I went on other actors wished me luck by saying _____ . It was then _____, the start of the show. I was waiting in the _____ . I heard one of the actors say the line that was my _____ ...

2. Write a sentence for each of the words in the Word cloud. Leave gaps where these words should be.

3. Swap your work with a partner. Ask them to complete your sentences while you complete their paragraph.

Developing your language – Shakespeare's English

Language has changed in 400 years since Shakespeare's time. Shakespeare used words with different meanings from the meanings they have today. Shakespeare also wrote in verse.

Read the following extract from Puck's speech and answer the questions.

Either I mistake your shape and making quite,
Or else you are that shrewd and knavish sprite
Called Robin Goodfellow. Are you not he,
That frights the maidens of the villagery,
Skim milk, and sometimes labour in the quern,
And bootless make the breathless housewife churn?

    From A Midsummer Night's Dream by William Shakespeare

1. What is the general meaning of this extract?

2. Identify the words that are no longer used today. Suggest a possible meaning for each word.

3. Does the verse improve the text of the speech?

Pronouns

Pronouns are used to replace nouns or noun phrases in a sentence, to avoid repetition of words. There are several types of pronoun.

1. **Personal pronouns** replace the name of a person or a thing. **Example:**

   The ants started crawling on my apple. They are so annoying! I couldn't shake them off.

2. **Possessive pronouns** replace a noun in a sentence but also show ownership. **Example:**

   These glasses are mine.

3. **Reflexive pronouns** are used to refer back to the subject. **Example:**

   She wanted to see where the noise came from for herself.

4. **Relative pronouns** are used to describe or limit the subject. **Example:**

   The song that we love was on the radio last night.

Using pronouns

Answer the questions below.

1. *I* and *they* are examples of personal pronouns. List the others.

2. Rewrite these sentences by replacing nouns with personal pronouns.

   a The theatre entertains my sisters greatly.

   b The writer of First Night had to act with Puck.

   c My mother and I sent some theatre tickets to Auntie Grace.

   d The members of the cast thanked all of our family.

3. **a** Practise acting the following speech out in a strong, angry voice:

   'It's mine I tell you, mine, mine! You're not having it because it's not yours. Those greedy people can't have it either. They think it's theirs, but it isn't. My sister's after it, but she's in for a shock when she discovers it's mine, not hers. Ha, ha! [*slightly madly*] Mine, mine, mine for ever and ever!

   b Copy this speech and circle the personal pronouns.

   c Name the other type of pronoun used in this speech.

> **Remember**
>
> When you say "my cat" or "your hat" or "their friends" you are using possessive adjectives, not pronouns.

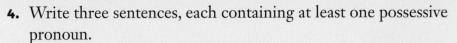
4. Write three sentences, each containing at least one possessive pronoun.

5. Identify the reflexive pronouns in the examples below.

   a When she is learning her lines she says them to herself.

   b Speaking for myself, I think she acted exceptionally well.

   c After the play, they treated themselves to several large burgers.

6. How is the spelling of a plural reflexive pronoun different from a singular reflexive pronoun?

7. Write a poem called 'Myself'.

8. a What type of pronoun are *who* and *which*?

   b When do you use *who* and when do you use *which*? Write two sentences as examples.

9. Join these sentences with relative pronouns.

   a He gave the script to his brother. His brother learned his lines in two days.

   b I had problems with the stage lighting. It kept on breaking the circuit.

💬 Speaking in pronouns on the phone

A friend is on the phone. Read the following one-sided conversation that you may overhear in this situation.

Answer the questions that follow.

> Hello, hello, **who** am I speaking to?
> **You** are too faint for **me** to hear.
> **You** wish to talk to **her**? **She**'ll answer for **herself**.
> **Your** voice is fading – ah, an invitation –
> By **ourselves**? For **us** at three o'clock?

1. Identify the types of pronoun in bold.

2. Can you understand the conversation fully? Explain your answer.

3. Suggest what the person on the other side of the phone may have said. Role-play the full conversation with a partner.

4. Improvise your own one-sided conversation in which you use pronouns instead of nouns to confuse others. Ask your listeners what the call is about.

A bored wife

In this extract from *Uncle Vanya*, by the Russian writer Chekhov, Helen is the new wife of the professor (Sonya's father) and finds country life boring.

1 *The drawing room of the professor's house. It is early*
   afternoon. Uncle Vanya and his niece Sonya are seated. Helen
   walks up and down, deep in thought.
   Vanya: [*pompously*] The learned professor has graciously
5   desired us all to assemble in the drawing-room
         at one o'clock today. [*Looks at his watch.*] It's a
         quarter to. He has some message for the world.
   Helen: It's more likely a business matter.
   Vanya: He never deals in such things. All he ever does is write
10   nonsense, grumble and feel jealous.
   Sonya: [*reproachfully*] Uncle!
   Vanya: All right, all right. I'm sorry. [*Points to Helen.*] Look at
         the way she goes around, nearly falling over from sheer
         laziness. [*sarcastically*] A charming sight, I must say.
15 Helen: Really, you keep on and on the whole day. Don't you ever
         get tired? [*miserably*] I'm **bored to death**, I don't know
         what to do.
   Sonya: [*Shrugging her shoulders.*] There's plenty to do if you
         wanted to.
20 Helen: [*irritably*] Well, what for example?
   Sonya: You could help to run the farm. You could do some
         teaching or nursing; there's plenty to do. For instance,
         before you and Father lived here Uncle Vanya and I used
         to go to market and sell our own flour.
25 Helen: [*solemnly*] I'm no good at that sort of thing, and besides
         I'm not interested. It's only in a certain kind of **earnest**
         novel that people go in for teaching and dosing peasants.
         And do you really see me suddenly **dropping everything**
         to run round nursing and teaching?
30 Sonya: What I don't understand is how you can help wanting
         to go and teach. You'd get used to it after a bit [*Embraces*
         her.] Don't be bored, dear. [*Laughing.*] You're bored, you
         don't know what to do with yourself and boredom and
         idleness are infectious.

                    From *Uncle Vanya* by Anton Chekhov

Word cloud

irritably

miserably

pompously

reproachfully

solemnly

sarcastically

Glossary

bored to death an exaggeration of being very bored

earnest novel a long book with a serious message

dropping everything stopping what someone is doing

Understanding

Answer the following questions.

1. Why were the three people in the drawing-room before one o'clock?

2. Explain how Helen was feeling and why.

3. What advice did Sonya give Helen to make her feel better? What did Sonya do?

4. Discuss the impression you get of each character.

 ## Word builder

1. Use the stage directions in the Word cloud to say the following quotations. Explain in each case how the stage direction affects the meaning of the extract.

   a "I'm no good at that sort of thing." Say it solemnly.

   b "The learned professor has graciously desired us all to assemble in the drawing-room at one o'clock today." Say it pompously.

   c "A charming sight, I must say." Say it sarcastically.

   d "Uncle! How can you say such a thing?" Say it reproachfully.

2. Read the extract from beginning to end, using the right expressions indicated by the stage directions.

Putting expression into your words

Improvise a short dramatic scene in a small group.

Each character chooses one of the following adverbs to describe the way they speak:

calmly   *angrily*   *nervously*   *dominatingly*
jokingly   *insultingly* *foolishly*   *confidently*

Your improvisation could take place at home, at school, or at the dentist's.

> **Remember**
>
> An adverb answers questions such as *when, where, why, how,* or *how much*. Adverbs can be used with adjectives or verbs.

Making words into plurals

> One, two, three,
> There's lots more of me!
> Most of us just add an 's',
> The other ones you mustn't guess.

You don't always simply add an *s* to make words into plurals.

Look at these examples.

Examples: *crash → crashes*

patch → patches

mass → masses

 What happens if singular words end in 'ch', 's', 'sh', 'x' or 'z'?

 The plural ends in 'es'

church → churches

Examples: *leaf → leaves*

loaf → loaves

 What happens if words end in 'f' or 'fe'?

 Most words change 'f' to 'ves'.

life → lives

Examples: *baby → babies*

body → bodies

 What happens if words end in a consonant followed by 'y'?

 Change them to 'ies'.

memory → memories.

Examples: *kilo → kilos*

radio → radios

stereo → stereos

hero → heroes

potato → potatoes

 What happens if words end in 'o'?

 Some change to 'oes' and others just add an 's'. You have to learn them!

However, there are exceptions to the rules. You have to learn these individually.

singular	plural
woman	women
person	people
roof	roofs
chief	chiefs
sheep	sheep
scissors	scissors

Spelling plurals

Use the rules above to spell the following sets of words.

1. wash   box   match   glass   branch   fox
2. wife   shelf   scarf   elf   half
3. spy   country   try   cry   boundary
4. piano   photo   tomato   volcano   tornado
5. man   tooth   foot   mouse

The plural spelling quiz

One person reads words from the following list for another to spell their plural forms. Continue until a word is spelled incorrectly. Move onto the next player. You do not have to write things down.

family	watch	bus	fly	fox
dictionary	baby	mother-in-law	clash	aunty
finish	flamingo	gallery	gas	genius
hiatus	housewife	injury	inquiry	jacuzzi
jelly	jetty	joy	kangaroo	kick-off
kiss	curry	lady	leech	avocado

Here are the answers for the questioner.

families	watches	buses	flies	foxes
dictionaries	babies	mothers-in-law	clashes	aunties
finishes	flamingos	galleries	gases	geniuses
hiatuses	housewives	injuries	inquiries	jacuzzis
jellies	jetties	joys	kangaroos	kick-offs
kisses	curries	ladies	leeches	avocados

Looking closely

English spelling is difficult because of the different origins of the language. Early words in the dictionary come from old English languages and French. Later words come from Latin and Greek. All have different spelling rules.

Punch and Judy show

Listen to the beginning of a traditional Punch and Judy puppet show. These shows have been popular in Europe since the 17th century, and are performed in the street for parents and their children. The presenter of the show is called the Bottler.

Word cloud

exhilarating

incorrigible

Glossary

cheer us up make us happy

gobstopper a very large sweet that stops you from talking

hold your ears back listen carefully

in unison all together

shan't colloquialism for 'shall not'

Understanding

Answer the following questions.

1. Why didn't Mr Punch answer when he was called?

2. Why was Mr Punch too miserable to sing a song?

3. What was so tiring about Mr Punch's dream?

4. What was Mr Punch going to do when he woke up?

5. Explain why Mr Punch came out in the end.

 Word builder

The Punch and Judy show is a reminder to use language to suit your audience. When writing for young children you shouldn't use long words if short ones would work just as well. **Example:**

"Mr Punch, you're incorrigible" can be made more simple by saying, "Mr Punch, there's no hope of turning you into a better person".

Here are some other things the Bottler says in this extract and elsewhere. Use a thesaurus to help you simplify the difficult words.

1. *We want an exhilarating song*
2. *You'd have been worked to an incorporeal shadow*

> **Remember**
>
> A thesaurus can be used to find words with similar meanings.

Developing your language – techniques used in speech

Look at the following extract from the show. Answer the questions that follow.

Bottler: You're miserable? What's the matter, Mr Punch?
Punch: Working too hard.
Bottler: Working too hard? What've you been doing?
Punch: Dreaming.
Bottler: Dreaming? That's not hard work.
Punch: Oh yes it is. I was dreaming I was working.
Bottler: Come on now, Mr Punch, dreaming you were working
doesn't make you tired.
Punch: Oh yes it does!

1. How does the Bottler make Mr Punch's words easier to follow? How does this help the audience?

2. Write a short scene later in the show where Mr Punch refuses to listen to the Bottler and only wants to play with his new stick.

Writing a scene from a play

Can you write a short play scene with an interesting situation, a setting, fascinating characters, and with stage directions?

Planning your scene

Use the following template to help you. Share ideas with others in your class and practise what your characters might say, or how they might say it.

Situation where the characters find themselves – and what is happening to them

Characters who think and speak differently

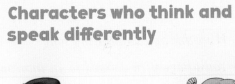

Title

Setting

Ending

Further guidance to writing a scene

Situations

Examples:

- three people stuck in a lift
- panic before leaving for a holiday
- walking into the wrong house by mistake
- trying to make yourself understood in a foreign country
- thinking mistakenly you have won a great deal of money

Characters

How will you make your characters different? These people and their relationships will make your play's storyline. Would it help to make one of your characters funny and the others more serious?

Stage directions

Use stage directions to describe the way your characters speak and what they do. When do they go offstage or when do they enter?

Setting it out

Playscripts are written out in a special way. Look back at page 88 and 93 to check how this is done.

Language

What will your characters say to make the storyline? Try improvising so that the words sound more natural, like in real speech. What happens if one character speaks politely while another speaks quite roughly?

How long?

The extract on page 88 is approximately 350 words in length. Aim to write about 300 words in your scene.

Performing your play

A play is a performance. Make sure that your play is entertaining to anyone watching it. Try also to write lines that are easy to remember for your actors.

Write your play using the guidance provided. Perform this in a group.

Progress check

1. Name two characters in Shakespeare's *A Midsummer Night's Dream* mentioned in *First Night*. [2 marks]

2. Explain the jobs of a producer and a prompter in the theatre. [2 marks]

3. If you were reading a play by Shakespeare what would you notice about the way it was written that is different from what you are used to? [2 marks]

4. What impressions did you have of the differences between the two women in the extract from *Uncle Vanya*? [2 marks]

5. In the history of the English language what has made spelling difficult? [2 marks]

6. Give the plural forms of *avocado*, *potato*, *person* and *sheep*. [4 marks]

7. Name four different types of pronoun. Give an example of each type. [4 marks]

8. Based on what you have learned about a Punch and Judy show, describe four unusual things about it. [4 marks]

9. What makes a play different from a story? Explain your answer. [4 marks]

10. From what you read in *First Night*, why might someone going on stage for the first time feel nervous and uncomfortable? [4 marks]

6

Reflecting on your learning – writing and performing a scene from a play

Focus on how to write a better playscript. Think about ways to improve any weaknesses. Ask yourself these questions.

7 Sizzling science

In this unit you will:

Explore
- space and the universe
- the limits of your imagination

Create
- a science fiction story
- different meanings by experimenting with prefixes

Engage
- with teenagers from different cultures
- with types of genre

Collaborate
- to go back in time with a partner
- to explore different genres

Reflect
- on the difference between science fiction and fantasy
- on what makes a successful story

Into the unknown

Science fiction is a genre where only the imagination limits the possibilities.

For it to be a true work of science fiction all ideas described must have a basis in scientific fact. Otherwise it's fantasy.

What was once science fiction is now science fact.

Thinking time

Use the images and quotations opposite to discuss:

1. Why is a good imagination important when writing a science fiction story?
2. Think of five inventions used today that would have been considered science fiction 100 years ago.
3. Think of a new invention that you would feature in a science fiction story.
4. Do you think there is life on other planets?

What is a genre?

The *Oxford English Dictionary for Schools* defines a genre as being 'a particular kind or style of art or literature'. Let's explore what this means. For a story to fit into the science fiction genre it should include some of these:

advanced technology not available today

set in an alternative past

voyages through space

time travel

spaceships

set in the future

other galaxies

robots

set on an alien planet

travel through dimensions

aliens

futuristic cities

set in a post-apocalyptic Earth

1. With a partner, list all the different kinds of genre you know.
2. On your own, choose one genre from your list and write down its features. Think of as many as possible.
3. Share your answers with your partner. What features are common to both genres? Why do you think this is?
4. Do you think that stories only ever include the features of one genre?

Speaking and listening

Discuss three important ideas that you think a science fiction story must have to be interesting and successful. Decide on their order of importance.

A discussion about science fiction

Listen to the discussion. Amin, Deepak and Hikari all give their reasons for really liking science fiction but for different reasons.

Understanding

Answer the following questions.

1. Complete this sentence: Amin learned about
_____ _____ in his _____ lesson and he was
happy because this is his _____ genre.

2. Choose three words that Hikari uses that show
she knows a lot about science fiction.

3. Match the speakers to the statements below.

   a "I like stories about robotics and novels set
   in futuristic cities."

   b "I like stories set far into the future but I
   also like the idea of living in an underwater
   city."

4. Why does Deepak use humour throughout the
discussion? Find some examples.

Developing your language – using semantic fields

A semantic field is a group of words that are all closely
connected to the same subject.

All the words in the Word cloud relate to ideas in the science
fiction genre.

Create your own semantic field. List all the words you can
think of on the subject of computers.

 ## Word builder

**Complete the sentences below using words from the
Word cloud.**

1. Travelling at the _____ is the quickest way to move between
solar systems.

Word cloud

alien

dystopian

extra-terrestrial

futuristic

robotics

speed of light

time travel

virtual reality

2. The _____ had four legs and heads and it was not human at all!

3. Studying the science of _____ will help us to create more useful machines in the future.

💬 Speaking and listening – taking part in a role-play

Amin begins the discussion by greeting his friends with "Hi guys". Later in the discussion Amin describes a reason for liking science fiction as really "cool". Both of these are examples of using colloquial language but they are acceptable in this discussion because it is an informal conversation amongst friends.

Answer the following questions.

1. Is the introduction "Hi guys" acceptable in the following situations:

   ● Meeting some friends in the playground

   ● Writing a letter to apply for a job

   ● In a business meeting

   ● Online in an Internet chat room

   ● When talking to your teachers?

2. Sometimes friends use their own informal semantic fields to create a bond between each other. This is Deepak talking to his friends online. Translate the words in bold into formal English.

   Yo buddies! I've just been **clocking** this **dude** on the **gogglebox** talking about what the world will look like in a hundred years' time. **Man** you'd be **awed** by what he said. It was so **cool**, I wish **ya** could have **eyed** it **yaselfs**.

3. With a partner, create a short role-play in response to the following scenario:

   You have just seen the latest science fiction film at the local cinema.

   Using as much informal language as you can, discuss your evening.

🔍 Looking closely

Colloquial language is used in conversation. If it is used in literature, it will probably be in a first-person narrative to create effect, or in dialogue. It shouldn't be used in formal writing.

Contractions in informal speech

Amin, Deepak, and Hikari conduct their friendship using social media, which means they do not always use language in the same way as they would if talking in a more formal situation.

Examples from their conversation:

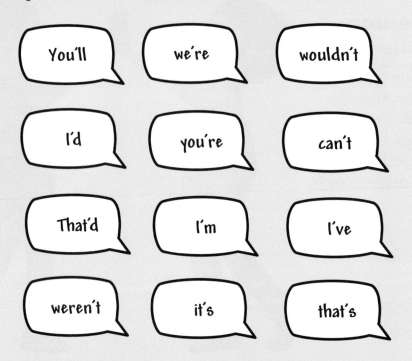

You'll   we're   wouldn't

I'd   you're   can't

That'd   I'm   I've

weren't   it's   that's

You'll is the contracted version of *you will*. The letters *w* and *i* have been left out to shorten the sound.

Won't follows a different convention. *Won't* is the contracted version of *will not*.

Answer the following questions.

1. Change the other contractions in the speech bubble into formal language.

2. Why do you think *won't* is not shortened to *willn't*? Try saying *willn't* out loud!

3. Write down other contractions you may use in informal situations. There's a clue in this sentence.

4. Use contractions to change these sentences into informal speech.

   a "We are going to miss the bus if you do not dress more quickly."

   b "I would have been on time for the bus if I had not stopped to look in that shop window."

The apostrophe

Apostrophes can be used in the following ways:

1. When using **contractions** to show where a letter, or letters, have been omitted.

   Example:

   did not → didn't   shall not → shan't

2. To show possession.

   Example:

   Deepak's jokes are really bad.

   The apostrophe is placed between the *k* and the *s* because there is only one of Deepak.

   However, for possessions belonging to more than one person or thing, the apostrophe is added after the *s*.

   Example:

   The three astronauts' air tanks were almost empty.

Using the apostrophe

Copy and complete the following by adding apostrophes to show possession or contraction.

1. Deepaks bus would have to travel a long way to reach Amins school.

2. Deepak has to do his homework and Hikaris grandparents are expecting her to visit them.

3. The two dragons claws were both really sharp.

4. The five players football kits were all dirty.

5. With only five minutes left before the end of the test all the students nerves were tingling.

6. Make the paragraph below more informal by adding contractions. You'll need to use 10 apostrophes.

   I love robots as they are so cool! I cannot wait to own one. That is my dream and I will save up until it is possible to buy one. Do not doubt me as I am determined to do it. It will take me years but that will make it even better. You should not expect me to change my mind.

In the Nick of Time

In this novel, Charlotte accidentally travels through a 'nick' (a small rip) in time, and finds herself trapped in a boarding school where no one will believe she is from the future.

In this extract Charlotte is taking part in a Maths lesson sitting next to Jack.

1   I sneak a peek at my watch, but I'm not quite sneaky enough. Jack leans across, **frowns** and **hisses**,

'What's *that*?'

'Watch.' I know why he's asking, of course. Digital. No such
5   thing in the fifties. Is *now* though, and what's more it works, unlike the moby.

'Let's have a dekko.' He's leaning too far across, Miss Stafford's bound to notice.

'That's not a watch,' he **growls**. 'There's no dial and no hands.
10   What is it *really*?'

'It's a watch,' I insist. 'A *digital* watch. You won't have heard of it, because it hasn't been invented yet.'

'Huh?' He gives me a funny look. 'Green van'll come for you, girl, any minute.'

15   I frown at him. 'What does that mean? *What* green van, Jack?'

He tuts. 'The one that takes you off to the nuthouse, of course.'

'Nuthouse?'

'Asylum. Lunatic asylum. Where they put people who've got things that haven't been invented yet.' He shakes his head. 'And once
20   you're in, nobody'll ever see you again. You or your digital watch.'

In this extract Charlotte is lying on an unfamiliar bed in the dormitory where all the girls sleep.

I don't sleep. I hardly ever lie on my right side, and on stretched canvas it's **excruciating**. My body manages to lie still but my
25   mind's **racing**. How did I get here, can I go back the same way, and what if I can't? How can somebody live before their parents are born? It's not possible. In 1952 I'm an impossibility, so I can't really be here. Which makes me ... what?

From In the Nick of Time *by Robert Swindells*

Word cloud

excruciating	hisses
frowns	racing
growls	

Glossary

boarding school a school where the students live during term time

dormitory a room where the students sleep

moby a slang term for a mobile phone

dekko a slang term meaning 'to look'

Understanding

Answer the following questions.

1. Why is Jack so fascinated by Charlotte's watch?

2. What do you think of Jack's reaction when Charlotte says she is from the future? Is it understandable?

3. Do you think Charlotte sees her journey back in time as an exciting adventure? Explain your answer.

Developing your language – using verbs for effect

When writing, your choice of verb can make a huge difference and can create a very particular effect.

1. Why do you think the author chose to write that Jack **'frowns and hisses'** instead of **'asks'**?

2. If Jack was asking in a more pleasant way, what verb could describe his actions?

 ## Word builder

The words in the Word cloud express emotions. Match them to their meanings.

1. make an angry sound like an 's'
2. moving very quickly
3. wrinkle your forehead in anger, worry, or disapproval
4. make a deep angry sound in your throat
5. causing intense suffering.

 ## Speaking and listening – taking part in a role-play

The idea that a character is suddenly placed in a previous time period allows the writer to explore interesting ideas about how far we might progress in the future.

In the first extract Charlotte's digital watch is used as a device to show how different technology was 60 years ago.

Role-play a conversation between two time travellers, one from the future, and one from the past.

Explain a piece of future technology to the time traveller from the past, who has no idea what it is.

Remember not to simply describe your piece of technology – you should also explain how it works and what it is used for.

Astronomical clock, Prague

Key concept

Prefixes and suffixes

A **prefix** is a letter or group of letters joined to the front of a word to alter its meaning in some way.

The following prefixes are used to change words to their opposite meanings:

un   dis   il   im   in   non   mis

However, beware in the case of words beginning with *un–*. Some words beginning with *un–* are simple adjectives.

Example:

united (joining together)

When letters are added to the end of a word to modify its meaning, we call this a **suffix**.

Remember

An adjective is a word used to give an attribute to or to qualify a noun. An adverb is different because it can modify the meaning of an adjective, or a verb, or even another adverb.

The prefix *un–*

Answer the following questions.

1. What happens when you put the prefix *un-* in front of the word *familiar*?

2. Does the same thing happen when you put *un-* in front of these words?

    a known   **b** lucky   **c** informed   **d** inhabited   **e** paid

3. Construct a rule to show how prefixes work in the five examples above.

4. Do these words also follow your rule when *un-* prefixes them?

    a freeze   **b** wrap   **c** wind

5. Do the following words fit your rule? Suggest why they may not. Is it to do with what kinds of words they are?

    a uncle   **b** unicorn   **c** unicycle   **d** uniform   **e** under

6. The following words begin with the prefix *un–*. Decide which are adjectives and which are verbs.

unready	unlock	unripe	unroll
unscrew	untangle	unseat	unseen
sizsteady	untrue	untie	unworn

More prefixes

Answer the following questions.

1. Experiment with different prefixes by adding them to these words. Write down all the words that can be made.

   a legal   **b** behave   **c** possible

   d correct   **e** honest   **f** active

2. Change the following sentences so they mean the opposite by adding a prefix to one word in each case.

   a What you said about my favourite movie was so helpful.

   b I cannot believe the television presenter showed so much respect to the movie actor.

   c The book I am reading is a work of fiction.

   d How can you be so logical when you put your point across?

   e I was informed by the driver that the bus would leave five minutes ago.

3. Add prefixes to the words in bold in the following passage to help this student explain why she dislikes science fiction.

I don't like science fiction stories because the ideas are so **probable** and I don't like fantasy because it is so **possible** and **logical**. **Believable** storylines are so annoying! I **trust** any story set on a different planet. These writers are **correct** in what they write. I think it should be **legal** to write fantasy stories as they are so **honest** and **true**. How **lucky** would I be to have to study these genres?

Welcome to a world beyond your wildest imagination!

FANTASMA

Your Favourite Fantasy Fun Park!

Voted number 1 in 2014

Now in its 20th amazing year!

Marvel at the magical **mythical** creatures Stare into the **scaly** serpent eyes of the **ghastly Gorgon**

(Safety glasses to be worn at all times)

New this season

Test your courage and try to answer the riddle of the **spiteful Sphinx**

(we cannot accept responsibility for the consequences of wrong answers)

Try tackling a **troublesome troll** in our incredible interactive 5D mega-attraction Fun for all the family

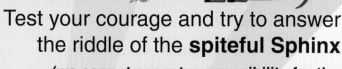

Kids – take a ride on Una our normally quite friendly unicorn.

(She just loves children – well, most of the time)

Smaug's Snacketeria

Savour your barbecued favourites in our ferociously fiery dragon restaurant.

(warning: Food may contain sulphur)

Thrills and spills   **Fear and frights**   **Fantasy favourites**

Tickets now available to buy online but hurry, they're going fast!

Understanding

The advertisement opposite is a poster for an imaginary theme park that features fantasy creatures from all around the world.

Answer the following questions.

1. Name three of the creatures in Fantasma.

2. Why might the park not be a safe place to visit?

3. What is the purpose of the writing in small print at the bottom of the poster?

4. What words and phrases suggest the poster is not meant to be taken too seriously?

5. Why does the advertisement for Fantasma belong to the fantasy genre and not science fiction?

Developing your language – using adjectives

Fiery and *scaly* are both adjectives used to describe the character of the mythical creatures. *Scaly* suggests snake-like and *fiery* suggests angry and aggressive.

Answer these question.

1. Change the adjectives in the following sentences to describe friendlier creatures:

   a The scaly eyes of the gorgon stared at me.

   b The fiery dragon stood in front of me.

2. Write down names of real creatures that you would describe as scaly.

3. Can you think of any fiery animals?

Developing your language – alliterations

List three examples of alliteration used in the advertisement to describe mythical creatures.

Word cloud

fiery	spiteful
ghastly	troublesome
scaly	

Glossary

mythical from imagination

gorgon a mythical creature whose look would turn anyone to stone

sphinx a mythical creature with the body of a lion and a human face

troll a mythical cave-dwelling creature often thought to eat humans

Key concept

Alliteration

Alliteration is the repetition of letters or sounds at the beginning of several words to create an effect.

Example:

marvel at the magical mystical creatures

Writing science fiction or fantasy

Plan and write a short story. The writing frame on the next page will help you to plan your ideas.

Use the following plot for your story.

It's the year 2120. Robots have become so advanced that they are part of our everyday lives.

Radek is a robot who belongs to the Dhawen family. They live on the edge of a forest, near a lake.

He looks after Sunil, the twelve-year-old only son of the Dhawens, when Sunil's parents are not around.

Sunil doesn't like robots and: _____ (the complication).

Sunil learns to trust the robot because: _____ (the resolution).

Some suggestions when writing this story:

- Before beginning to write, decide on the verb tense you will use and who is going to narrate the story.

- The beginning could explain why Sunil doesn't like robots.

- The complication could possibly be caused by Sunil disobeying the robot.

- The subsequent action is up to you!

- The ending sees Sunil learning to trust the robot.

In your group, use the same characters, setting and basis for the story, but create your own plot twist, solution and ending.

Try to include specialist vocabulary of possible new technology from 2120 to turn your story into science fiction.

 # Having a group discussion

Before you start your planning and writing, this statement:

All successful stories have some common and important features.

Discuss this in a group and decide on what these important features are.

Hint: Think about how you, as a reader, like to be kept interested when reading a book.

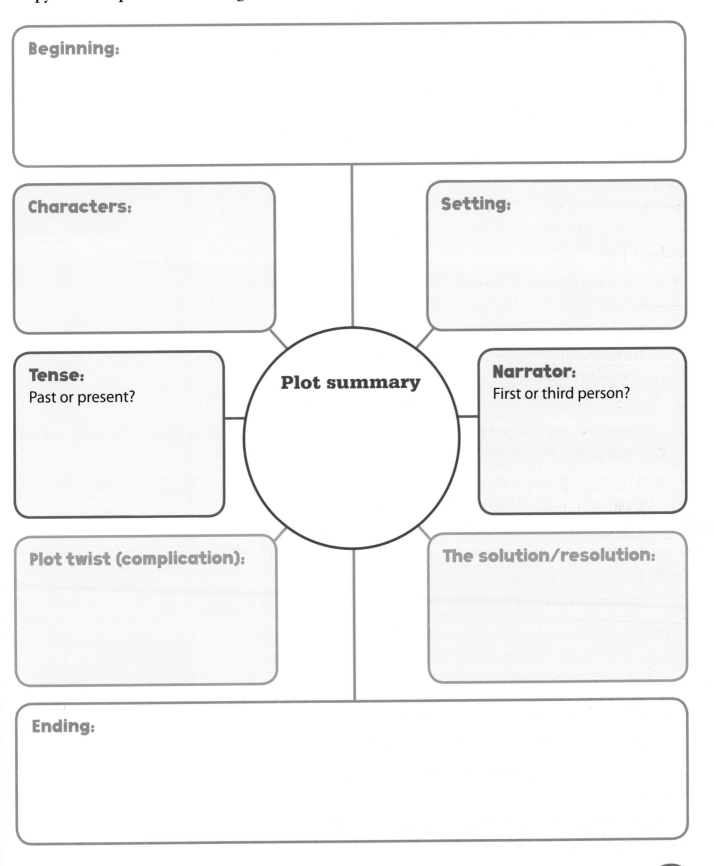

Structuring and drafting your writing

Copy and complete this writing frame.

Beginning:

Characters:

Setting:

Tense:
Past or present?

Plot summary

Narrator:
First or third person?

Plot twist (complication):

The solution/resolution:

Ending:

Checking your progress – unit test

1. Why are new inventions important in science fiction stories? Give two reasons. [2 marks]

2. Name two features you might expect to find in a science fiction story. [2 marks]

3. Science fiction stories often include journeys. Give two examples of where these journeys might take you. [2 marks]

4. Name two differences between the genres of science fiction and fantasy. [2 marks]

5. Why is it important to use a writing frame when planning a story? [2 marks]

6. What is a genre? Give three examples of genres other than science fiction or fantasy. [4 marks]

7. In the extracts from *In The Nick of Time* the characters' actions are further explained using verbs to communicate their feelings. Can you remember two of the verbs used? Explain why each is effective. [4 marks]

8. Thinking about the Fantasma advertisement, what devices should this kind of literature include to make it effective? Name two devices used in the poster and give examples for each. [4 marks]

9. Explain why a good imagination is so important for successful science fiction and fantasy writers. [4 marks]

10. When planning a story, what choices do you have to make regarding the narrative voice and tense, and what difference do your decisions make to the way you write? [4 marks]

7

Reflecting on your learning – planning and writing a short story

Copy and complete the following table.

When writing a short story, I can:	I fully understand	I think I do	I'm not really sure
use a writing framework to plan my story			
think of the main idea for the story			
write a plot summary			
create interesting characters			
know what my ending will be			

My action plan for improvement

Choose one of your weaker areas. Think of improving this area as a journey between planets.

- What is my journey's destination?
- How will I carry out my mission?

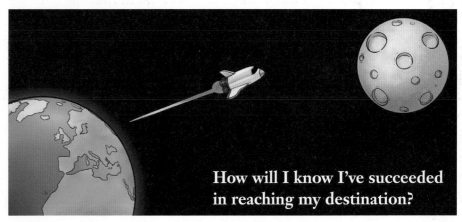

How will I know I've succeeded in reaching my destination?

In this unit you will:

Explore
- life in an Indian village
- life in Roman times

Collaborate
- to decide on a definition of history
- to role-play life in an ancient Roman house

Create
- a biography of someone else's life
- dialogue, and experiment with using punctuation

Engage
- with words from Latin to see how English words are formed
- with a member of your family to learn about their past

Reflect
- on life in a house by the seaside 2000 years ago
- on grandparents talking about their lives 50 years ago

The Roman Forums, Italy

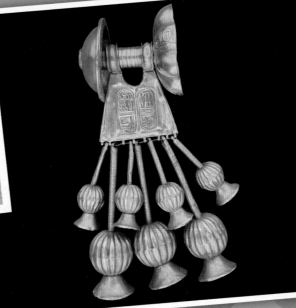

I don't like history: it's only a list of dates and endless battles.

History starts the day before I was born and then goes backwards in a straight line!

The more you read about how people lived in the past, the more you realise they were just like us, only they didn't have cars and computers.

Thinking time

1. Look at the images on the opposite page. Discuss how they are related to history.
2. Look at the quotes on the same page. Do you agree or disagree with any of them?
3. Add your own quote about history.

Speaking and listening

Discuss each of the three quotations in turn and then give your views of what history is all about. Try to do this in just one sentence.

History in the news

Read the following newspaper item and answer the questions.

http://www.bbc.co.uk/news/uk-politics-31929772

1 Yesterday, **historian** Yelda Yo, an expert in the prehistory of our oldest region and the President of the National Society of Historians, opened an exhibition of artefacts in Gotensk. She described it as a '**historic** occasion'. Yelda
5 was very enthusiastic about this event and said that she had been interested in **prehistoric** findings ever since she was a child. It was not until she was older that she realised some of this was very useful **historical** evidence.

1. Identify the common root word for the words in the Word cloud. (In Old French it is *estoire*.)
2. Find two words in the extract that are derived from the Latin word for *out*. (The Latin word for *out* is *ex*.)
3. Find a word in the extract that is derived from the Latin word for *hold*. The Latin word is *habere*. This is more of a challenge!

Word cloud

historian   historical
historic   prehistoric

 Word builder

Complete the following sentences using words from the Word cloud.

1. My father, who was a _____, studied the Greek civilisation.
2. Dinosaurs were _____ beasts.

Looking closely

Root words are words that have a meaning of their own but can be added to. They are useful in working out what a longer word means. *Artefact* has two root words from Latin – *arte* and *factum* – meaning 'the ability to make something.

Autobiography

Read the following extract from an autobiography, telling the story of a girl's personal history.

Earliest Memories – A Faraway Land

1   Raghunathpur was a typical Indian village: a rustic, **ancient** backwater of dusty, uneven streets and **crumbling** old houses made up of mud-bricks covered in masks of cement. It boasted no great achievements or personalities. All that existed was a
5   hard-working community who expected or desired little from life other than a healthy existence and a proud family. It was very rural and so, inevitably, it was very poor. I spent the first years of my life in that **archaic** Bengali village.

  The three of us – my mother, my sister and I – lived in the two-
10   roomed house of my father's parents, and the rooms were both very small – so tiny that a double bed could barely be fitted in. Still we knew nothing of any other way of life and lived there quite contentedly.

  Waking up, I would begin a series of curious actions that I would
15   perform every morning – a sort of routine that built up and seemed inevitable in the daily, **repetitive** life of the village. Jumping out of bed, my sister and I used to search around in the darkness of our single room for some little bags. The **cramped** room had one, very small opening which could be loosely classified as a 'window'
20   but which for the most part let in little of the radiant beams of the midday sun, always so high in the sky. Having found our bags, we used **to totter out** on to the open veranda which led to our grandparents' room. We shrieked in our high Bengali tones like young eaglets. Soon afterwards, our grandfather's **wrinkled prune-**
25   **dry face** would appear round the **scratchy** old door. Smiling, he would drop some unknown morsels in our bags. Somehow we all received great pleasure from that strange, simple routine.

  At about nine o'clock my sister would leave for school. I would undergo a reflex action; I would cry and moan like a wounded
30   dog to follow her and just occasionally, I would be allowed to trot after her. We lived in an area of the village known as 'Nandura' and it was a short walk down the **dust-sedimented lane** lined with sun-baked houses with exteriors that from a distance looked like leopard skins thanks to the presence of round, dark cowpats

Word cloud

ancient	repetitive
archaic	scorching
cramped	scratchy
crumbling	

Glossary

cackle laughing in a way that sounds like hens or geese

dust-sedimented lane a road that has many layers of dust

to totter out to walk very carefully

wrinkled prune-dry face so dried out that the face looks like a dried plum

lining the sand-coloured walls, cooking solid in the **scorching** heat of the day. The lukewarm wind blew dust into our faces from time to time, and large, loose swarms of mosquitos flew around in their irregular formations. There was the **cackle** of children playing, and men walked slowly down the lanes, their pure, white shirts and pyjamas shining in the golden daylight.

From *Earliest Memories – A Faraway Land* by Subhajit Sarkar

Understanding

Subhajit's story is part of an autobiography, which is written by her and tells the story of her childhood. If someone else wrote about her life it would be a biography.

Answer the following questions.

1. What does Subhajit tell you about:
   - **a** the village
   - **b** the weather
   - **c** the house she lived in
   - **d** her grandfather?

2. Did Subhajit come from a rich family? How can you tell?

3. How did you feel when you read this autobiographical account?

Developing your language – using words to create effect

Writers will sometimes use words to create effect. The choice of words is very important if you want to make the reader respond in a particular way.

Answer the following questions using the words in the Word cloud.

1. What do these words have in common?

2. Are they positive, 'feel good' words, or are they negative?

3. Which two words are the most powerful?

4. Add two similar words that would fit in the Word cloud.

🧩 Word builder

Write antonyms for each of the words in the Word cloud.

Sentences and conjunctions

Types of sentences

Simple sentences contain one verb and end with a full stop. **Example:**

> I live in Raghunathpur.

Simple sentences can be joined using **coordinating conjunctions**, such as *and*, *but*, and *so*. **Example:**

> The streets in Raghunathpur were uneven. The houses were made of mud bricks.

> The streets in Raghunathpur were uneven and the houses were made of mud bricks.

Two simple sentences joined using coordinate conjunctions become a **coordinated sentence**.

Simple sentences

Identify the simple sentences from the list below.

1. It was very rural and so inevitably it was very poor.

2. The lukewarm wind blew dust in our faces.

3. We lived in a two-roomed house.

4. There was a cackle of children playing and men walked slowly down the lanes.

Creating coordinated sentences

Answer the questions below.

1. Use the conjunctions *and*, *but*, and *so* to join the sentences below. Use a different conjunction for each pair of sentences.

   a   There were windows with small openings. They hardly let in any light.

   b   Sometimes I was told I could follow my sister to school. I used to trot after her happily.

   c   Our house was very tiny. It had only two, cramped rooms.

2. Create four simple sentences that can be added to the extract.

3. Make a single, coordinated sentence from the sentences you have written for Question 2.

4. What rule have you learnt about coordinated sentences?

Commas in dialogue

Dialogue

Dialogue is formed when a conversation between two or more people is written down. You show when their words begin and end by using speech marks, commas, and full stops. **Example:**

"Time to get up," whispered my sister.

"It's too dark," I replied, "and I can't find my little bag."

"Here it is, with mine," was the reply. "Come on, let's wake up Grandfather."

Focus on commas

Insert commas where you think they should be used in the following dialogues. Do not add other punctuation.

1. "Good morning children" said Grandfather appearing round the scratchy old door.

2. "Good morning Grandfather" I replied in a pleading voice "and can I go with my sister to school today?"

3. "Maybe" murmured Grandfather putting our treats in our bag "and maybe not."

💬 Speaking and listening

1. Role-play a conversation that Subhajit and her sister could have had during the day. Use the right tone of voice to convey the meaning.

2. Note down where you are pausing in this dialogue.

3. Write some of the dialogue down, inserting commas in the correct places.

A house in Pompeii

Let's visit a Roman house built by the sea in Pompeii 2000 years ago. Here's a letter the owner might have written to a friend.

1 Hi Lucius
I'm sorry I haven't written to you for what must seem ages. I've got exciting news –
I've just moved into my new house here in
5 Pompeii. It's by the seaside and there's a lovely **vista** of Mount Vesuvius behind the town. I'm ready for visitors. Summer's on its way and I know you'll want to escape from Rome for a couple of months. All that heat
10 and dust! What d'you say?

My house is small but well-designed, and it's just by the public baths. There are two rooms at the front. They are shops for my businesses. You enter between them and
15 walk into the main meeting place. And then you'll see my masterpiece – a **magnificent** art gallery. I've spent a great deal of money on many fine paintings of Greek mythology, here and around the house. I have pictures of
20 Zeus himself, and of Helen of Troy.

You'll enjoy feasting in the dining room. A craftsman has made me a fine, **sturdy** table for food. You should try out the couches around the walls: they are the comfiest
25 in Pompeii. When you come, I'll give you **delicacies** such as lettuce, snails, eggs, barley cake, and a few equally delicious surprises. We'll feast till morning!

A **spacious** courtyard leads from the
30 meeting place and there's a relaxing view of a small garden and a little shrine. The little statue of a creature carrying fruit will make you laugh.

Of course, my customers come to the house. I was afraid that someone would steal 35 the paintings or wander into my private rooms. So I had this brilliant idea! Just as they enter the house, they step onto a design in the floor. It's most lifelike – a ferocious, bloodthirsty creature with layers of pointed 40 teeth that would tear you to shreds. It seems to leap out at you though it's held back by a strong, iron chain. I think even I am afraid of this monster. Well, it'll keep the criminals away! 45

When you visit, there's no need to bring your strongest sandals because the paths here are very smooth and **manicured**. I hope to see you very soon.

Publius

Word cloud

delicacies	spacious
magnificent	sturdy
manicured	vista

Understanding

> **Key concept**
>
> ### Inference
> When you form an opinion or work something out based on what someone says or does, it is called inferring. The skill you are developing is **inference**.

1. Will Lucius want to come and stay in Publius' house? Why?
2. Is Publius wealthy? Explain your answer.
3. Publius is very pleased with himself for building his house. Write down three words to describe him as a person.
4. Suggest why Publius hasn't written to Lucius for so long.
5. What can you infer from the painting on Publius' floor?

Developing your language – connotations of words

> **Key concept**
>
> ### Connotations
> A **connotation** is an idea or feeling which a word gives you, in addition to its meaning.
> Words can be classified into three basic groups:
> - those with a positive connotation
> - those with a negative connotation
> - neutral words.

negative

positive

neutral

Answer the questions using words in the Word cloud.

1. What connotations do these words have?
2. Can any be used with a negative connotation?
3. Write down three words with positive connotations.
4. Write three neutral words.

 Word builder

Use words in the Word cloud to answer these questions.

1. How does each word imply that Publius' house is special?
2. Find five other words Publius uses to tempt Lucius to visit.
3. Use these words to write new sentences in a different context – but still related to a period of history.

Using contractions

Spoken language uses different constructions from those used in formal writing. Examples from Publius' letter:

- "I've got exciting news…"
- "I know you'll want to escape…"
- "What d'you say?"
- "We'll feast till morning!"

Pompeii sunset

Look at Publius' letter and answer these questions.

1. Match the following statements to one of the examples of spoken language above.

   a He uses an exclamation mark to make what he writes seem exciting and dramatic.

   b Instead of saying 'I have' he shortens it to make it sound like speech.

   c He asks Lucius a question so as to give him a chance to respond.

   d He tempts Lucius by suggesting he knows what is going on in Lucius' mind.

2. Find four other examples from the letter where Publius uses contractions. For each of these, state what the intended effect is.

Remember

If the register is informal – for example, in a letter to a friend – then it would be normal to use some contractions.

Throughout the letter, Publius uses contractions to make his writing sound friendlier.

Examples:

- I have not = I haven't
- I am = I'm
- You will = You'll
- Do you = D'you

More contractions are shown in the circles on the right. Match the contractions to the original phrases.

No it is not
It is
You are

They're
You're
We'll
No it isn't
It shouldn't
It's

We will
It should not
They are

Changes in meaning

Not all contractions end up with the same meaning as the two original words. For example, you might say "I'm pleased to see you." However, "I **am** pleased to see you" means something slightly different.

Suggest possible meanings to the examples below. Rewrite the sentences using contractions.

- You are looking splendid tonight.
- I will attend to it later, and I have already told you that.
- She will not be happy to see you.
- I have a very serious meeting to attend.

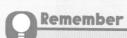

Remember

If you want to emphasise something, it is better to avoid contractions and to use the two words.

Role-play

One of you will pretend to be Publius and the other will be Lucius. Lucius has arrived at Publius' house and will be spending a week with Publius.

Decide which day you are going to hold your conversation. Will it be on the first day, a few hours after Lucius has arrived? Or will you hold your conversation halfway through the week, perhaps after a very large feast? Or maybe your talk can take place towards the end of the week, as Lucius is about to leave.

Use informal language and contractions in your conversation.

Talking about the past

A conversation with Ghada's grandparents

In this dialogue, 12-year-old Ghada talks to her grandparents about their lives 50 years ago.

Glossary

everything is laid on it's an easy life for some people

mind you pay attention please

it took ages it took a very long time

in the back of beyond in a very rural area

Understanding

Answer the following questions.

1. Do Ghada's grandparents suffer from boredom, and how do you know this?

2. Even though the grandparents were relatively poor as young adults, what could have made things much worse for them?

3. Do you think Ghada's grandparents had a good life when they were young? Explain your answer.

4. How do the grandparents differ in their views of modern life?

Looking closely

A cliché is a phrase that is so overused it no longer has any meaning.

Developing your language – using expressions

Carry out the following activity.

1. Practise saying each of the expressions in the Glossary box so that you can hear the sound of the expression.

2. Write down some more expressions that you use or that you have heard other people use.

3. What is a cliché? When do you think an expression becomes a cliché?

Using your thesaurus

Key concept

Synonyms

A dictionary tells you the meaning of words. A thesaurus gives a list of words with similar meanings. These words are called synonyms.

Examples of words from Ghada's conversation with their synonyms:

Energy: liveliness, vigour, vitality, life

Rusty: corroded, weather-beaten, damaged, shabby

Wrecked: destroyed, smashed up, demolished, crushed

Answer the following questions.

1. Which of the alternative words to *energy*, *wrecked* and *rusty* would you rather use? Why?

2. Nana says "Your granddad and I were real young farmers. Oh yes, full of energy." Suggest a synonym to use without changing the meaning.

3. Nana says "We did have a rusty old bicycle." Are any of the words from the thesaurus as good as *rusty* or do they change the meaning?

4. 'If the storms came and wrecked the crops' is a strong statement. Do any of the alternatives convey the idea as strongly?

5. Write down other synonyms for *energy*, *wrecked*, and *rusty*.

Planning and writing a biography

Autobiography versus biography

Subhajit's story (which you read on page 116) is part of an **autobiography**, written by her and telling the story of her childhood. If someone else wrote about her life it would be a **biography**.

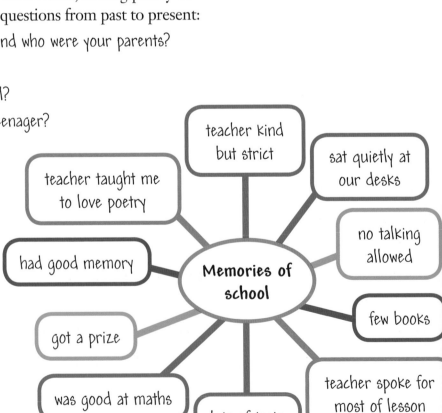

Ghada found that her grandparents had a lot to say about their life 50 years ago.

Choose an older person you know well to write their biography.

Plan the questions you will ask and listen carefully to what they say about their life. Be polite and don't ask very personal questions. If possible, make a recording to listen to when you are drafting your work.

Planning your writing

Decide what questions to ask. Write them down, leaving plenty of space to add responses. Examples of questions from past to present:

- When and where were you born, and who were your parents?
- What are your earliest memories?
- What are your memories of school?
- What was it like for you to be a teenager?
- What did you do when you left school?
- What are you proudest of achieving so far?
- What do you think are the main differences between your early life and life nowadays?

Your notes might look like this:

Select only the key information or the facts that are most interesting, when you are ready to start writing.

teacher kind but strict

sat quietly at our desks

teacher taught me to love poetry

no talking allowed

had good memory

Memories of school

few books

got a prize

teacher spoke for most of lesson

was good at maths

lots of tests

Structuring your work

Biographies are usually written in chronological order – from past to present. Each set of memories should form a separate paragraph. Each paragraph should start with a topic sentence. The topic sentence tells you what the paragraph is about and is often a link to the paragraph that came before. Example plan for your biography:

Paragraph 1: Introducing your subject

An introduction to who you are interviewing. **Example:**

> My grandmother's name is Ludmilla and she was born in Russia 70 years ago.

This sentence introduces the whole biography using basic facts.

Paragraph 2: First idea – memories

Used to set out the first idea from your notes. **Example:**

> Her earliest memories go back to when she was three years old, but they do not form any pattern.

This tells the reader that the memories that follow might not be in a particular order.

Paragraph 3: An extension of the previous idea

Example:

> One memory that is particularly strong was the first day she went to school.

This sentence tells the reader how this paragraph links to the previous one, and what it will include.

Presenting your biography

Biographies often use:

- photographs
- extracts from original material related to the subject
- quotations.

Include at least one of these when you finalise your biography.

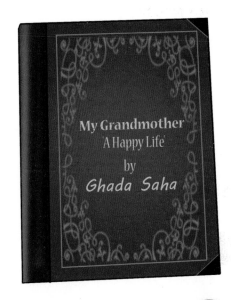

My Grandmother
'A Happy Life'
by
Ghada Saha

Progress check

1. Summarise the meaning of the word *history* in
12 words. **[2 marks]**

2. Identify the effect of using the following words
in a short story:
raining, heavily, soggy, slippery, flooding **[2 marks]**

3. Think of two simple sentences about history. Now
join them together in a single sentence, using a
conjunction. **[2 marks]**

4. In what sense are autobiographies and biographies
history? **[2 marks]**

5. Write the topic sentence for a paragraph on how
the school history trip suffered its worst day. **[2 marks]**

6. Write two sentences where punctuation changes
their meaning. Write each sentence twice: once with
punctuation, and once without. **[4 marks]**

7. Give four examples of how Publius tried to convince
Lucius to come and stay at his new house. **[4 marks]**

8. Write down two things that Ghada thought about
her grandparents. How do you know this? **[4 marks]**

9. Write down four features of a biography that would
make it appealing. **[4 marks]**

10. Give two pros and two cons of using a thesaurus. **[4 marks]**

Reflecting on your learning – speaking and listening in small groups

My speaking and listening skills when I am working in small groups	Strong and I can help others	Good and I have no real worries	OK but more work is needed	I need to work hard to improve
Preparation for discussion-based group work				
Contributing to discussions in small groups				
Keeping track of the discussion and listening to the contributions of others in the group				
Encouraging and guiding other people to develop their points				
Summarising the findings of the group and reporting back to the class				
Learning from other groups and not just my own				

Focus on the areas where you most need to improve. Think about improving these skills on a timeline.

Write down what you can do today so that your speaking and listening skills are improved.

Write down things you can do in the next few weeks to help you achieve your goal.

How will you know whether you have succeeded in reaching the end of your timeline?

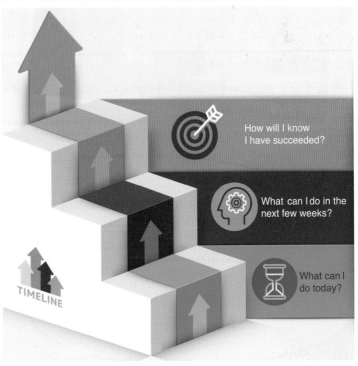

TIMELINE

How will I know I have succeeded?

What can I do in the next few weeks?

What can I do today?

In this unit you will:

Explore
- boundless deserts
- craggy mountains

Create
- a haiku
- a longer poem

Engage
- with ideas and events
- from the past

Collaborate
- to make pictures from poems
- to read poems aloud together

Reflect
- on reading and studying poetry
- on your skills as a writer of poems

A poem is a painting that speaks.

Poetry: the best words in the best order.

Poetry is all that is worth remembering in life.

Thinking time

1. Look at the quotations on the opposite page to help you think about poetry.

2. Discuss the meaning of 'the best words in the best order'.

3. How can a poem be like a 'painting that speaks'?

4. How does 'all that is worth remembering about life' help you to understand what poets write about?

Speaking and listening

Do you know some poems already?

What do you like or dislike about them?

What different sorts of poetry have you read?

Developing your language – the language of poetry

Poetry often uses ways to make words seem stronger, more lively, more sensitive, and most importantly, more effective. Two devices that feature in this unit are syllables and alliteration.

Remember

Alliteration occurs when two or more words close to each other start with the same letter or sound.

Key concept

Syllables

Syllables are different parts of a word. **Examples:**

like has one syllable

thunderstorm has three syllables

Poems are made up of lines of roughly the same number of words, and often each line has exactly the same number of syllables.

Answer the following questions.

1. Count the total number of syllables in your name.

2. Count the syllables in the names of three towns or cities in your country.

3. How might knowing about syllables help in reading or writing poetry?

4. Think of two alliterative phrases that can be used to describe the weather in each of these photos.

5. Can you describe yourself, using alliteration? Write this down.

6. Can you think of any occasions where alliteration might not be effective? Explain your answer.

'The Ballad of Sir Patrick Spens'

This extract is from a ballad that is hundreds of years old. A ballad is a traditional song or poem that tells a story.

It tells the story of a voyage taken by Sir Patrick Spens, whose ship was caught in bad storm on the way to Norway, wrecking the ship and causing all on board to die.

Glossary

league a measure of distance

silken made from silk

twine string or thread

ne'er never or not

The Ballad of Sir Patrick Spens

1   They had not sailed a league, a league,
    A league but barely three,
    When the sky grew dark, and the wind blew loud,
    And **gurly** grew the sea.

5   The **anchors** broke and the **top-masts** snapped,
    It was such a deadly storm;
    And the waves came o'er the broken ship
    Till all her sides were torn.

    "O where will I get a good sailor
10 To take my **helm** in hand,
    Till I get up to the tall top-mast
    To see if I can spy land?"

    "O here am I, a sailor good,
    To take the helm in hand,
15 Till you go up to the tall top-mast,
    But I fear you'll ne'er **spy** land."

He had not gone a step, a step,
A step but barely one,
When a bolt flew out of the good ship's side,
And the salt sea it came in.

"Go fetch a web of silken cloth,
Another of the twine,
And wrap them into our good ship's side,
Let not the sea come in."

They fetched a web of silken cloth,
Another of the twine,
And they wrapp'd them into the good ship's side,
But still the sea came in.

And many was the feather-bed
That floated on the **foam**;
And many was the good lord's son
That never more came home.

Anonymous

Word cloud

anchors	helm
foam	spy
gurly	top-masts

Understanding

Answer the following questions.

1. Why did Sir Patrick Spens want to climb up the tall top-mast?

2. Explain why he did not do this.

3. What do 'silken cloth' and 'feather-bed' tell you about the people on board the ship?

4. Look at the whole poem and explain how the ship's situation worsened.

 Word builder

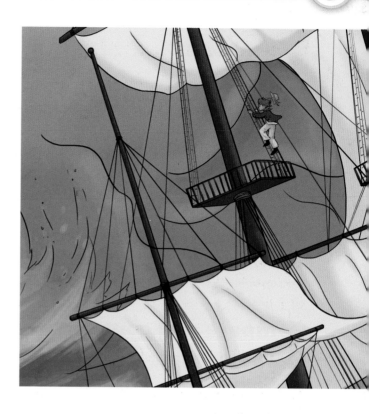

All the words in the Word cloud tell you about the ship and the stormy sea.

Gurly is not in the dictionary, but the words around it say that the sea grew, the weather was dark and the wind was blowing. You can guess therefore that gurly means something like wild or rough.

Look at the words in the Word cloud in the context of the poem. Answer these questions.

1. For each word, use the context to suggest its meaning.

2. Check your definitions using a dictionary. Write down the correct definition for each incorrect definition.

3. Draw an outline picture of the ship in the storm. Label your picture using each of the six words in the Word cloud.

4. Make a list of other words you know that are parts of a ship. Use a dictionary to help you.

5. Describe the wind and waves using similes and metaphors.

 Remember

The words that come before and after a word that help to identify the word's meaning are called its context.

 Describing the storm

Imagine you are a sailor in another ship that passes the wreckage after the storm stops.

Give a spoken report of the storm, including what you saw, in a conversation with the king.

Comparisons

When you **compare** things you look for similarities and differences. **Example:**

> You can compare two students by saying that one is quiet in class and the other is always answering questions.

When you compare two things to find their differences, it is called a **contrast**.

Compare and contrast

Read the poem below and compare it to 'The Ballad of Sir Patrick Spens'. Answer the questions that follow.

Storm!

I ran to the forest for shelter,
Breathless, half **sobbing**;
I put my arms round a tree,
Pillowed my head against the rough **bark**.
"Protect me," I said. "I am a lost child."
But the tree showered silver drops on my face and hair.
A wind sprang up from the ends of the earth;
It **lashed** the forest together.
A huge green wave thundered and **burst** over my head.
I prayed, **implored**, "Please take care of me!"
But the wind pulled at my cloak and the rain beat upon me.

Katherine Mansfield

1. What effects do the two storms have on the people in the poems?
2. What do the two poems have in common?
3. How do the two poems differ?
4. Is there a pattern in the words used in these two poems and the lengths of the lines? Explain your answer.
5. Which poem do you prefer, and why?

Word cloud

bark	lashed
burst	sobbing
implored	

Structuring poems

The Ballad of Sir Patrick Spens

This poem is a ballad that tells a story. It is also the lyrics of a song. The story is told in the order of events. Each verse tells a new part of the story.

Answer these questions.

1. What important event is missing from the ballad? Why do you think this is?

2. How many verses would you need to complete the story? What events would the extra verses tell?

3. Write an extra verse to add to this poem. This verse can be added in any position.

Storm!

'Storm!' is a poem without any particular shape, rhymes, or fixed number of syllables in each line. Poems like this are called 'free verse'.

Answer the following questions.

1. What does Katherine do to protect herself?

2. How do you know that the wind and the rain get worse as the poem goes on?

3. How does the poem show you Katherine's fear and emotions as the storm gets worse?

4. Comment on the following statements. Do you agree, or disagree? Explain your answer.

   a "'Storm!' is much more complicated than 'The Ballad of Sir Patrick Spens'."

   b "The poem 'Storm!' should be made into verses."

   c "The lines in 'Storm!' are unequal in length and there are no rhymes. This cannot be a poem.

Looking closely

Stating events as they happen, from the earliest event to the most recent, is stating them in chronological order.

Remember

Narrative poems tell stories. Descriptive poems describe things, for example, the wind, the rain, or the trees.

Imagining the scene

Imagine you are crossing a desert and you see a pile of stones in the distance. You go up to it and investigate. Something is carved into one of the stones — what could this be?

Shelley wrote the following poem around 200 years ago. At the time, exciting new discoveries were being made about Egypt's past.

Ozymandias

1   I met a traveller from an antique land
    Who said: Two **vast** and trunkless legs of stone
    Stand in the desert. Near them on the sand,
    Half sunk, a shatter'd **visage** lies, whose **frown**
5   And **wrinkled** lip and **sneer** of cold command
    Tell that its **sculptor** well those passions read
    Which yet survive, stamp'd on these lifeless things,
    The hand that mock'd them and the heart that fed.
    And on the **pedestal** these words appear:
10 "My name is Ozymandias, king of kings:
    Look on my works, ye Mighty, and despair!"
    Nothing beside remains: round the **decay**
    Of that **colossal** wreck, boundless and bare,
    The lone and level sands stretch far away.

Percy Bysshe Shelley

Understanding

Answer these questions.

1. The statue of Ozymandias is a ruin. List the words within the poem that tell you this.

2. How do you know that the sculptor did not like Ozymandias?

3. What do you think of the writing at the pedestal of the statue? Explain your answer.

4. Say the last three lines aloud.

   a What is special about 'boundless and bare' and 'lone and level'?

   b How do these phrases help you to understand the poem better?

Word cloud

colossal	sneer
decay	vast
frown	visage
pedestal	wrinkle
sculptor	

Developing your language – punctuation and poetry

Poets are usually very careful to use punctuation to make their meanings clear.

Complete the following activities.

1. Simple sentences in poems such as 'The Ballad of Sir Patrick Spens' only need simple punctuation. Read the following verse and decide where commas and full stops should go. Explain your answer.

   > He had not gone a step a step
   >
   > A step but barely one
   >
   > When a bolt flew out of the good ship's side
   >
   > And the salt sea it came in

2. 'Ozymandias' is a more complicated poem. A bigger range of punctuation is required for this poem to make sense. Read the following:

   > My name is Ozymandias king of kings
   >
   > Look on my works ye Mighty and despair

   Compare this version with the original on the previous page.

   a Why are quotation marks (" ") needed in the original version?

   b Why are there commas round 'ye Mighty'?

   c Why did Shelley use a capital letter for 'Mighty'?

   d Why is there an exclamation mark at the end?

3. After 'king of kings', there is a punctuation mark called a colon (:). It separates two sentences, but their meaning is connected. In one sentence Ozymandias tells you how powerful he is. After the colon he says all other mighty rulers should despair because he is the greatest.

   a Find other colons used in this poem. Why does Shelley use them?

   b Read the whole poem aloud. Pause when you see punctuation – but do not stop if there is no punctuation at the end of a line.

Remains of a statue in honour of an Egyptian king

Grammar in prose and poetry

Poetry does not have to obey the rules of prose. With prose you would expect to write sentences of different lengths, but in poetry your ideas will often have to fit the shape of the poem and sometimes even the number of syllables in a line.

'Ozymandias' is a 14-lined poem called a sonnet. Each line must contain ten syllables.

Answer these questions.

1. Read this version of the beginning of 'Ozymandias' in prose:

> A tourist told me this story. He said that he visited the site of a ruined statue in the middle of the desert. The statue had no body, but there were two gigantic legs still standing, and he saw the fragments of a face which was half-buried in the sand. The look on the face was cruel.

   a What do you notice about the lengths of the four sentences?

   b Look at 'Ozymandias' again. What do you notice about the lines? How easy is it to make them into sentences?

   c Choose another part of the poem to make one complete sentence.

2. Poetry is usually written in sentences, but some poems break the rules. Read this extract from a descriptive nature poem.

> Ancient, grey mountains
> giants against sunlight
> in darkening Western skies
> until tomorrow's dawn.

   a What is this poem about?

   b Rewrite this poem in prose.

   c Identify three differences between the two versions.

Analysing poetry

Read this short poem by Alfred Tennyson.

> **The Eagle**
>
> He clasps the crag with crooked hands;
> Close to the sun in lonely lands,
> Ring'd with the azure world, he stands.
>
> The wrinkled sea beneath him crawls;
> He watches from his mountain walls,
> And like a thunderbolt he falls.
>
> Alfred Tennyson

← An eagle perches on a bare rock high on a mountain.

← The eagle is so high waves in the sea look like tiny lines. It suddenly swoops down like thunder.

A group of students are discussing this poem. One of them criticises the poem:

- Firstly, it is bad grammar. You don't say 'and like a thunderbolt he falls' you say 'he falls like a thunderbolt'.

- Secondly, you can't try to pretend the eagle is like a human. An eagle is 'it' and it hasn't got hands – it's got claws or talons.

- Thirdly, whoever heard of a sea having wrinkles and crawling? This describes babies, not seas!

Answer the following questions.

1. Think about what this person says. Write a response to each of his criticisms.

2. Do you think that poetry should follow rules? Explain your answer.

 **Looking closely**

Poetry is different from prose. Sometimes the order of the words is different in poetry and there may be sentences without verbs. Poets adapt grammar to fit their needs.

Studying poems at school

Preena and Guilang go to different schools and are talking about studying poetry. The three poems they mention were all written over 100 years ago.

Listen to their conversation carefully, making notes to help you remember what is being said.

Understanding

Answer these questions.

1. Why doesn't Guilang like poetry lessons?

2. Is there anything that Guilang likes about poetry?

3. How did Preena describe Guilang's attitude to homework?

4. What sorts of poem does Preena like, and why?

5. From their conversation, what can you infer about Preena and Guilang? List three ideas.

Word cloud

by heart   put you off

make fun of   that's tough

Developing your language – spoken expressions

People often use informal language in conversations.

Answer the following questions.

1. List three informal expressions you use when talking to your friends.

2. Do you use these expressions when talking to your teacher? Explain your answer.

3. Suggest why we use informal expressions in conversation.

Word builder

Complete these sentences using phrases in the Word cloud.

1. I'm sorry you've had a bad day. _____!

2. Don't _____ me. You know I'm easily embarrassed.

3. I don't want to _____ but they say the new teacher's very strict.

4. Don't keep on complaining to me. I know what you're going to say _____.

Developing your language – writing a character report

Read Preena's and Guilang's school reports below.

dishonest · untidy · troublesome · insolent · idle · insulting · naughty

Mirang School: report
Guilang is an obedient, polite boy, but he is rather lazy and is unenthusiastic about work. He is popular with his friends and energetic when it comes to football practice. He represents the school and is committed to the team's success.

Kota School: report
Preena is very lively and extremely confident in speaking and listening activities. She is kind to others and understanding to those in trouble. She has taken pride over her work and is imaginative, especially in her writing and her artwork. She can be a little impatient when she gets something wrong.

unsmiling · uncommunicative · timid · proud · arrogant · teacher's pet · unhappy · spoilt

Your character is all the things that make you what you are as a person. Guilang is rather lazy and unenthusiastic.

Your personality is like character, but is more what people immediately notice about you. Preena is kind and understanding.

Write a short school report for one of the two students in the pictures.

Haikus

Haikus are Japanese poems with only three lines. **Example:**

> Forest at midnight
>
> Dark leaves drip warmest liquid
>
> Giant moths zoom by

There are five syllables in the first line, seven in the second, then five in the final line.

Understanding haikus

Read the following haikus to answer the questions that follow.

Ⓐ
> Deep snow has fallen
> Frost clutches at blades of grass
> Feet slide on ice paths

Ⓑ
> Brown bears are hungry
> Invading trash cans for food
> Beware their embrace

Ⓒ
> Rivers snake eastwards
> Flowing from the frozen hills
> Glaciers in motion

1. Identify the subject of each haiku.

2. Pick the most appealing word in each haiku. Explain your choice.

3. What message is each haiku trying to send?

 # Writing haikus

Write a haiku about an aspect of nature.

Choose your words carefully – the first word you think of may not be the best.

Use the pattern for writing haikus:

introduce the topic → appeal to the senses → send your message

       Line 1   Line 2   Line 3

✏️ Writing a longer poem

Take the theme of your haiku and expand it into a longer poem.

Your poem should have three verses with four lines in each verse. The first line of your haiku can become the title of your poem. **Example:**

In 'Forest at midnight' the first verse could be about the strange lights, the plants and trees, and the warm, sweet smells. The second verse could be about the sounds and the movements of insects, birds, and animals. The third verse could be about how you felt if you were there at the time, or perhaps what is going to happen next.

Use the following guidance to help you:

- Use short lines with approximately the same number of syllables, but add a longer line or a very short one sometimes, for effect.
- Explore a different idea in each of the three verses.
- Use alliteration to create atmosphere.
- Choose the liveliest words you can think of to engage your reader's imagination.
- Introductions are not required in poetry.
- Make sure you include an ending.

Starting a poem

Here are the beginnings of two famous poems. Both use short lines.

> Tyger, tyger burning bright
> In the forest of the night –

> I know some lonely houses off the road
> A robber'd like the look of

Ending a poem

There are many different ways to end a poem. Look back at the endings of poems in this unit to help you.

Progress check

1. How many syllables are in these words?
   identification   *manufacture*.   [2 marks]

2. Give two words that rhyme with *crawls*.   [2 marks]

3. What is a narrative poem? Give an example of a narrative poem that you studied in this unit.   [2 marks]

4. Can you remember where Tennyson's eagle perched? What could it see far below it?   [2 marks]

5. What does *chronological* mean? Since *meter* means measure, suggest the meaning of *chronometer*.   [2 marks]

6. What is alliteration? Find an alliterative word to go in front of 'brother', 'sister' and 'parents'.   [4 marks]

7. How many lines does a haiku poem have and how many syllables are there in each line?   [4 marks]

8. What do you do when you compare two things? Identify three things you look for when comparing poems.   [4 marks]

9. What does *character* mean and how can you form an opinion about someone's character when you are reading a story? [4 marks]

10. Describe four differences between prose and poetry.   [4 marks]

Reflecting on your learning – poetry race!

Take part in this race to the finish!

At each stage decide whether you are in the lead, in the middle, catching up or just getting started.

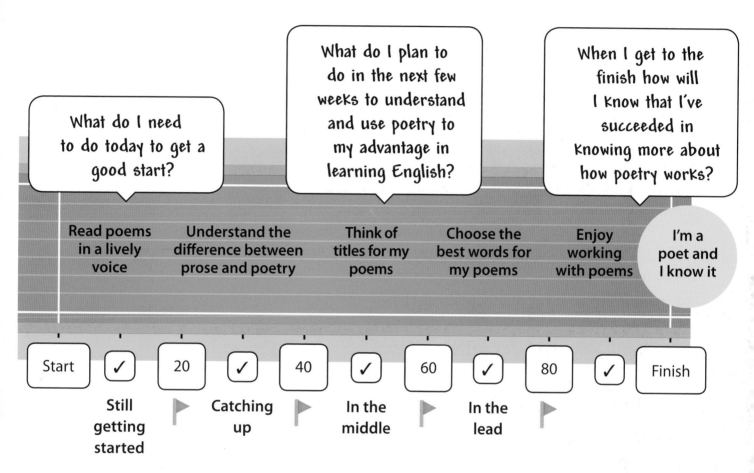

This is a longer extract from The Lastling, the adventure story you encountered in Unit 1. If you're feeling confident with your reading, have a go at reading this extract before answering the Understanding questions on p149.

No Way But Up

'Where did you come from?' Tahr hardly knew, these days, whether he was speaking words out loud, in his own tongue or English, or in Geng-sun's way with hands, the angle of his head, his eyebrows, eyes, and shoulders. He must have said it out loud, because Paris answered.

'She came down … from … up there.' Paris had edged to the cave mouth, steadying herself against the tree roots as she looked up. She swallowed. 'Oh my …' she said. Above them, the grey rock leaned out, glistening with wet, hung with fringes of ivy from the overhanging edges. Underneath them, the river swirled. Paris clutched the tree and closed her eyes. 'Oh my … she said again.

Geng-sun looked at her mildly, puzzled, then swung past her, leaning out over the drop by one hand, pointing upwards as casually as if they'd asked for directions on a city street. *Let's go*, her look said.

Tahr was out beside them now. *No, no!* He shook his head, gesturing to Paris, then himself. Even a mountain goat wouldn't contemplate it. Geng-sun didn't seem to grasp the problem, till Tahr mimed *Trembling … Frightened … Slipping … Falling*. He signed to the rope ladder. *Can't we go down?*

Geng-sun's *No!* had no words, but it came like a shout—a shake of her head, her eyes shut tight a moment and a sideways chop of the hand. End of argument. There were some more gestures, but she didn't need to spell it out. Down there, somewhere, were the rebels—out of sight now, but they might be back any moment. Once down in the gorge, they would be in a trap. *No*. Geng-sun wasn't arguing. She was telling them, with all the instincts of a sometimes-hunter, sometimes-hunted thing. *We go up.*

'It's impossible. Tell her!' Paris whispered. But Geng-sun was answering her already—with a swift look to the coils of ladder … to herself … to *up there*. Her hands did a knot dance, indicating: *Take the end … and tie it … safe.*

And so that was the plan. There was no other. Geng-sun was in action quickly, rifling through the spare stores that the rebels had up there. Any scraps of food went in the hide pouch at her belt. And there was a rope—the one they'd looped round Tahr's neck. Geng-sun made that small quick startle movement Tahr had come to recognize as *having an idea*. Uncoiling enough for her climb, she tied one end of the rope to the rope ladder, clamped the other in her big strong teeth, and then she was off, up, flowing from tree-root to foothold to tiny cracks not big enough to take a finger ... flowing upwards as if her big bones had no weight. She threaded a way between overhangs and crumbling clumps of vegetation with the ease of a snake through grass, and she didn't look back. Tahr did not call after her. He knew that every muscle, every sense of hers was in the climbing, just like every inch of her was running when she ran or eating when she ate. Besides, he had a job of his own to do. He had to sell this plan to Paris.

When the rebels hauled her up into the cave, it had been so hard not to react. But if he had called out, as he wanted, if he'd even smiled, that would have been it, for both of them. And yet Tahr's heart was thumping as he struggled to keep his face expressionless.

Paris looked younger now—a girl, not a woman. Hurt and shaken, she wasn't one of the gods. She was a girl a little older than him, from a country where the food they give them makes them grow up big and pale. That sprawling swaggering ease of hers had gone, and her air of command. She was frightened.

At the first look up the rock, her whole body had gone rigid, and her head was shaking: *No, no, no* ... Now, as he explained what was going to happen, she relaxed a little ... just enough to have a doubt. 'Don't you think I'm better off with these guys?' she said, glancing down at the unconscious Gurung. 'I mean, if I'm a hostage ... they won't want to ... lose me, will they? Pop's got money ... him and Franklin ...' Her voice trailed off, as the ambush played itself out again inside her mind. And she seemed to remember something from a year or two ago, about some hostage on the news ...

'I know what you're going to say,' she said, hopelessly.

Tahr looked at her. She was hesitating, and the more she hesitated, the harder it would be. 'These men are desperate,' he said. 'They are angry and afraid. Very bad combination.' There was a jerk on the rope, and the ladder started to unfurl itself and clatter up. Paris glanced at it and went pale.

'Your uncle,' said Tahr. 'We can find him, if he has escaped.'

The rope ladder went taut, and after a moment there was a little hissing in the air, and the end of the spare rope snaked back down. Tahr caught it and gave it a firm tug. 'There,' he said, as if this was a plan they'd already discussed. 'We tie this round you ... so. Then she can hold you if ...' He stopped. Just the word *fall* might be too much for her.

Easy. All she had to do was ... trust the *yeh-teh*. With her life.

Tahr had looped the rope around her, more than once, just in case, and three or four extra knots at the end to be sure. 'Now,' he said gently. 'You climb.'

'Only if ... if you climb too. If you ... talk to me.'

'Talk?' Tahr said. 'About what?'

'Anything. Please!' said Paris. 'I just need to know you're there.'

Twice she nearly blacked out—she almost wished that she could—and she found herself clamped to the ladder, her arms through the rungs and hugging it with all her strength. Eyes shut, she felt the rung against her cheek and it was all right, it would be all right as long as she could stay right here and never move again. Except her calf muscles were starting to ache and tremble. But when she tried to shift her weight at all, the rope ladder swung away and she froze and clung again.

Tahr was there, as he'd promised—just below her—and his voice came in a steady mutter, one of his chants in Buddhist language. As long as it was his voice, Paris didn't care.

She mustn't look down. She mustn't think the obvious—that if the rebels came back now, they'd be dangling up there, helpless. Target practice.

'Please,' said Tahr. 'My hands are tired. You must climb on.'

Once, Paris's foot slipped, rolling off the rung. The rope around her waist snapped tight, at once, as if Geng-sun could see her, which she couldn't, or could read her every movement through the twine. For a moment she dangled, and her free foot lashed out. 'Still!' said Tahr sharply, as he caught it. He guided it back to its rung.

The last bulge in the rock face was the hardest, with trailing creepers and crumbling earth raining down into her face and eyes. The rope was tight against the rock, and she had to squeeze her fingers in behind it to get hold. She knew her knuckles were bleeding, but she could not feel them.

Tahr spoke again, in a strained voice. 'You must go faster. Please.'

Then Paris was over the overhang, with Geng-sun hauling her in, hand over hand. She lay full length, panting, with the feel of cold rock and crumbly lichen on her cheek. Already, Geng-sun was stepping over her and climbing down, right to the edge, reaching down to where Tahr must be. Dimly, Paris realized what Tahr had been saying all that time. He wasn't roped, climbing up behind her, and he'd had to wait each time she got scared, hanging on … Now Geng-sun held the rope with one hand and reached down with the other, and gradually Tahr's head appeared. He was grey with exhaustion and the ledge was not in reach, not quite … As his fingers slipped, Geng-sun's hand clamped his wrist and held him. It was only a second, but enough to give him strength. He clutched at the ladder again and dragged himself onward, and there he was suddenly, flat out on the ledge beside her like a landed fish.

From *The Lastling* by Philip Gross

Understanding

1. Compare the way Paris' movements and actions are described with how Geng-sun moves. Why does the writer create this comparison?

2. How does Tahr express his and Paris' fear at the plan to climb?

3. How does this extract show that language is more than just words?

Language and literacy reference

Active voice versus passive voice – Verbs are active when the subject of the sentence (the agent) does the action. Example: The shark swallowed the fish. Active verbs are used more in informal speech or writing.

Verbs are passive when the subject of the sentence has the action done to it. Example: The fish was swallowed by the shark. Passive verbs are used in more formal writing such as reports. Examples: An eye-witness was interviewed by the police. Results have been analysed by the sales team.

Sometimes turning an active sentence to passive, or vice versa, simply means moving the agent:

- The shark (agent and subject) + verb = active
- The fish (object) + verb = passive

Adjective – An adjective describes a noun or adds to its meaning. They are usually found in front of a noun. Example: Green emeralds and glittering diamonds. Adjectives can also come after a verb. Examples: It was big. They looked hungry. Sometimes you can use two adjectives together. Example: tall and handsome. This is called an adjectival phrase.

Adjectives can be used to describe degrees of intensity. To make a comparative adjective you usually add –er (or use more). Examples: quicker; more beautiful. To make a superlative you add –est (or use most). Examples: quickest; most beautiful.

Adverb – An adverb adds further meaning to a verb. Many are formed by adding -ly to an adjective. Example: slow/slowly. They often come next to the verb in a sentence. Adverbs can tell the reader: how – quickly, stupidly, amazingly; where – there, here, everywhere; when – yesterday, today, now; how often – occasionally, often.

Adverbial phrase – The part of a sentence that tells the reader when, where or how something happens is called an adverbial phrase. It is a group of words that functions as an adverb. Example: I'm going to the dentist **tomorrow morning** (when); The teacher spoke to us **as if he was in a bad mood** (how); Sam ran **all the way home** (where). These adverbials are called adverbials of time, manner and place.

Alliteration – Alliteration occurs when two or more nearby words start with the same sound. Example: A slow, sad, sorrowful song.

Antecedent – An antecedent is the person or thing to which the pronoun refers back. Example: President

Alkira realised that his life was in danger. 'President Alkira' is the antecedent here.

Antonym – An antonym is a word or phrase that means the opposite of another word or phrase in the same language. Example: shut is an antonym of open. Synonyms and antonyms can be used to add variation and depth to your writing.

Audience – The readers of a text and/or the people for whom the author is writing; the term can also apply to those who watch a film or to television viewers.

Clause – A clause is a group of words that contains a subject and a verb. Example: I ran. In this clause, I is the subject and ran is the verb.

Cliché – An expression, idiom or phrase that has been repeated so often it has lost its significance.

Colloquial language – Informal, everyday speech as used in conversation; it may include slang expressions. Not appropriate in written reports, essays or exams.

Colon – A colon is a punctuation mark (:) used to indicate an example, explanation or list is being used by the writer within the sentence. Examples: You will need: a notebook, a pencil, a notepad and a ruler. I am quick at running: as fast as a cheetah.

Conjugate – To change the tense or subject of a verb.

Conditional tense – This tense is used to talk about something that might happen. Conditionals are sometimes called 'if' clauses. They can be used to talk imaginary situations or possible real-life scenarios. Examples: If it gets any colder the river will freeze. If I had a million pounds I would buy a zoo.

Conjunction – A conjunction is a word used to link clauses within a sentence such as: and, but, so, until, when, as. Example: He had a book in his hand when he stood up.

Connectives – A connective is a word or a phrase that links clauses or sentences. Connectives can be conjunctions. Example: but, when, because. Connectives can also be connecting adverbs. Example: then, therefore, finally.

Continuous tense – This tense is used to tell you that something is continuing to happen. Example: I am watching football.

Discourse markers – Words and phrases such as on the other hand, to sum up, however, and therefore are called discourse markers because they mark stages along an argument. Using them will make your paragraphs clearer and more orderly.

Exclamation – An exclamation shows someone's feelings about something. Example: What a pity!

Exclamation mark – An exclamation mark makes a phrase or a short sentence stand out. You usually use it in phrases like 'How silly I am!' and more freely in dialogue when people are speaking. Don't use it at the end of a long, factual sentence, and don't use it too often.

Idiom – An idiom is a colourful expression which has become fixed in the language. It is a phrase which has a meaning that cannot be worked out from the meanings of the words in it. Examples: 'in hot water' means 'in trouble'; It's raining cats and dogs.

Imagery – A picture in words, often using a metaphor or simile (figurative language) which describes something in detail: writers use visual, aural (auditory) or tactile imagery to convey how something looks, sounds or feels in all forms of writing, not just fiction or poetry. Imagery helps the reader to feel like they are actually there.

Irregular verb – An irregular verb does not follow the standard grammatical rules. Each has to be learned as it does not follow any pattern. For example, catch becomes caught in the past tense, not catched.

Metaphor – A metaphor is a figure of speech in which one thing is actually said to be the other. Example: This man is a lion in battle.

Non-restrictive clause – A non-restrictive clause provides additional information about a noun. They can be taken away from the sentence and it will still make sense. They are separated from the rest of the sentence by commas (or brackets). Example: The principal, who liked order, was shocked and angry.

Onomatopoeia – Words that imitate sounds, sensations or textures. Example: bang, crash, prickly, squishy.

Paragraph – A group of sentences (minimum of two, except in modern fiction) linked by a single idea or subject. Each paragraph should contain a topic sentence. Paragraphs should be planned, linked and organised to lead up to a conclusion in most forms of writing.

Parenthetical phrase – A parenthetical phrase is a phrase that has been added into a sentence which is already complete, to provide additional information. It is usually separated from other clauses using a pair of commas or a pair of brackets (parentheses). Examples: The leading goal scorer at the 2014 World Cup – James Rodriguez, playing for

Columbia – scored five goals. The leading actor in the film, Hollywood great Gene Kelly, is captivating.

Passive voice – See active voice.

Person (first, second or third) – The first person is used to talk about oneself – I/we. The second person is used to address the person who is listening or reading – you. The third person is used to refer to someone else – he, she, it, they.

- I feel like I've been here for days. (first person)

- Look what you get, when you join the club. (second person)

- He says it takes real courage. (third person)

Personification – Personification can work at two levels: it can give an animal the characteristics of a human, and it can give an abstract thing the characteristics of a human or an animal. Example: I was looking Death in the face.

Prefix – A prefix is an element placed at the beginning of a word to modify its meaning. Prefixes include: dis-, un-, im-, in-, il-, ir-. Examples: impossible, inconvenient, irresponsible.

Preposition – A preposition is a word that indicates place (on, in), direction (over, beyond) or time (during, on) among others.

Pronoun – A pronoun is a word that can replace a noun, often to avoid repetition. Example: I put the book on the table. It was next to the plant. 'It' refers back to the book in first sentence.

- Subject pronouns act as the subject of the sentence: I, you, he, she, it.

- Object pronouns act as the object of the sentence: me, you, him, her, it, us, you, them.

- Possessive pronouns how that something belongs to someone: mine, yours, his, hers, its, ours, yours, theirs.

- Demonstrative pronouns refer to things: this, that, those, these.

Questions – There are different types of questions.

- Closed questions – This type of question can be answered with a single-word response, can be answered with 'yes' or 'no', can be answered by choosing from a list of possible answers and identifies a piece of specific information.

- Open questions – This type of question cannot be answered with a single-word response, it requires a more thoughtful answer than just 'yes' or 'no'.

- Leading questions – This type of question suggests what answer should be given. Example: Why are robot servants bad for humans? This suggests to the responder that robots are bad as the question is "why are they bad?" rather than "do you think they are bad?" Also called loaded questions.

- Rhetorical question – Rhetorical questions are questions that do not require an answer but serve to give the speaker an excuse to explain his/her views. Rhetorical questions should be avoided in formal writing and essays. Example: Who wouldn't want to go on holiday?

Register – The appropriate style and tone of language chosen for a specific purpose and/or audience. When speaking to your friends and family you use an informal register whereas you use a more formal tone if talking to someone older, in a position of authority or who you do not know very well. Example: I'm going to do up the new place. (informal) I am planning to decorate my new flat. (more formal)

Regular verb – A regular verb follows the rules when conjugated (e.g. by adding –ed in the past tense, such as walk which becomes walked).

Relative clause – Relative clauses are a type of subordinate clause. They describe or explain something that has just been mentioned using who, whose, which, where, whom, that, or when. Example: The girl who was standing next to the counter was carrying a small dog.

Relative pronoun – A relative pronoun does what it says – it takes an idea and relates it to a person or a thing. Be careful to use 'who' for people and 'which' for things. Example: I talked to your teacher, who told me about your unfinished homework. This is my favourite photo, which shows you the beach and the palm trees.

Restrictive clause – Restrictive clauses identify the person or thing that is being referred to and are vital to the meaning of the sentence. They are not separated from the rest of the sentence by a comma. With restrictive clauses, you can often drop the relative pronoun. Example: The letter [that] I wrote yesterday was lost.

Semi-colon – A semi-colon is a punctuation mark (;) that separates two main clauses. It is stronger than a comma but not as strong as a full stop. Each clause could form a sentence by itself. Example: I like cheese; it is delicious.

Sentence – A sentence is a group of words that expresses a complete thought. All sentences begin with a capital letter and end with a full stop, question mark or exclamation mark.

- Simple sentences are made up of one clause. Example: I am hungry.

- Complex sentence – Complex sentences are made up of one main clause and one, or more, subordinate clauses. A subordinate clause cannot stand on its own and relies on the main clause. Example: When I joined the drama club, I did not know that it was going to be so much fun.

- Compound sentence – Compound sentences are made up of two or more main clauses, usually joined by a conjunction. Example: I am hungry and I am thirsty.

Good writers use sentences of different lengths to vary the pace of their writing. Short sentences can make a strong impact while longer sentences can make text flow.

Simile – A simile is a figure of speech in which two things are compared using the linking words 'like' or 'as'. Example: In battle, he was as brave as a lion.

Simple past tense – This tense us used to tell you that something happened in the past. Only one verb is required. Example: I wore.

Simple present tense – This tense is used to tell you that something is happening now. Only one verb is required. Example: I wear.

Standard English – Standard English is the form of English used in most writing and by educated speakers. It can be spoken with any accent. There are many slight differences between Standard English and local ways of speaking. Example: 'We were robbed' is Standard English but in speech some people say, 'We was robbed.'

Suffix – A suffix is an element placed at the end of a word to modify its meaning. Suffixes include: -ible, -able, -ful, -less. Example: useful, useless, meaningful, meaningless.

Summary – A summary is a record of the main points of something you have read, seen or heard. Keep to the point and keep it short. Use your own words to make everything clear.

Synonym – A synonym is a word or phrase that means nearly the same as another word or phrase in the same language. Example: shut is a synonym of close. Synonyms and antonyms can be used to add variation and depth to your writing.

Syntax – The study of how words are organised in a sentence.

Tense – A tense is a verb form that shows whether events happen in the past, present or the future.

- The Pyramids are on the west bank of the River Nile. (present tense)

- They were built as enormous tombs. (past tense)

- They will stand for centuries to come. (future tense)

Most verbs change their spelling by adding –ed to form the past tense. Example: walk/walked. Some have irregular spellings. Example: catch/caught.

Topic sentence – The key sentence of a paragraph that contains the principal idea or subject being discussed.